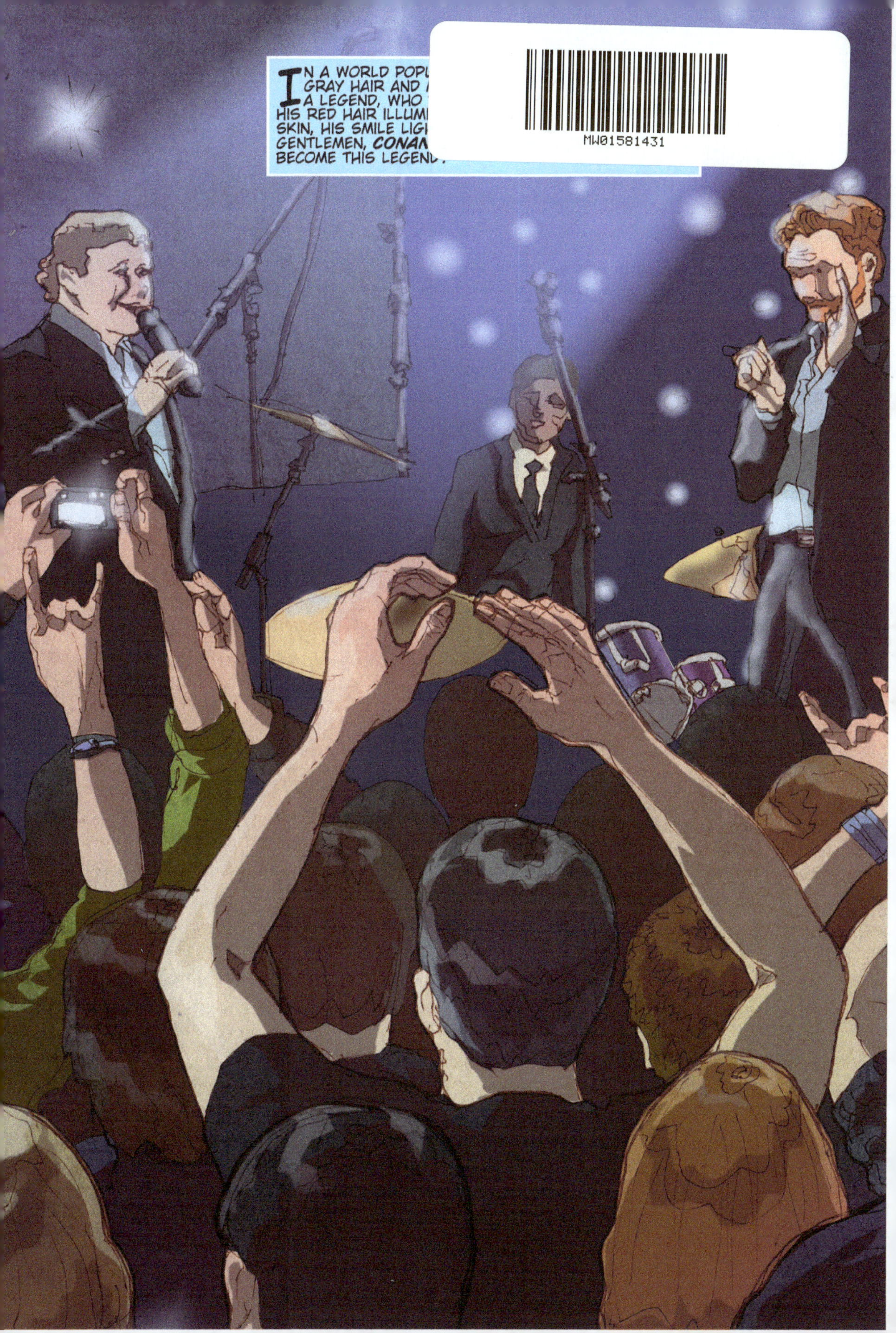
IN A WORLD
GRAY HAIR AND
A LEGEND, WHO
HIS RED HAIR
SKIN, HIS SMILE
GENTLEMEN,
BECOME THIS LEGEND

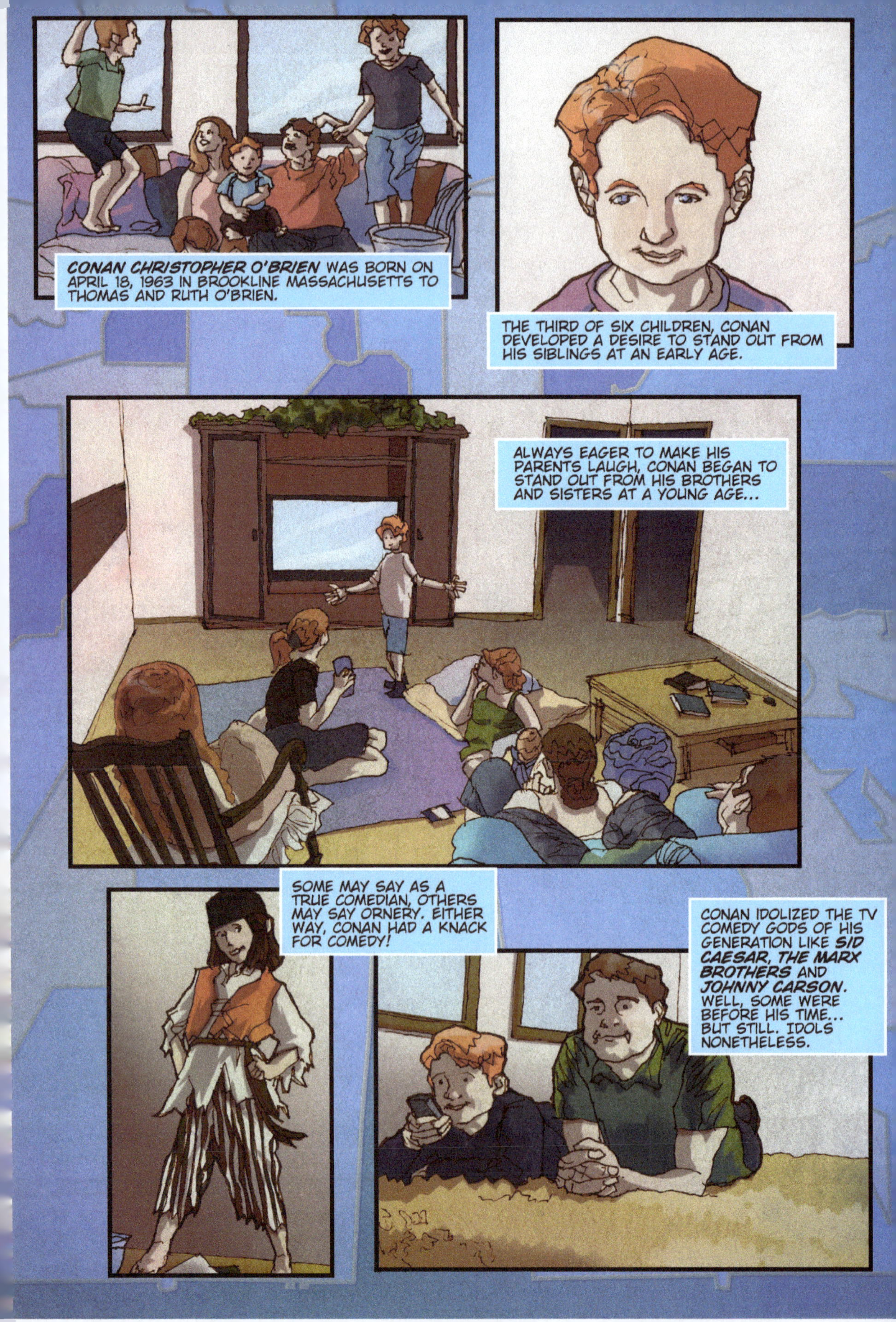
CONAN CHRISTOPHER O'BRIEN WAS BORN ON APRIL 18, 1963 IN BROOKLINE MASSACHUSETTS TO THOMAS AND RUTH O'BRIEN.
THE THIRD OF SIX CHILDREN, CONAN DEVELOPED A DESIRE TO STAND OUT FROM HIS SIBLINGS AT AN EARLY AGE.
ALWAYS EAGER TO MAKE HIS PARENTS LAUGH, CONAN BEGAN TO STAND OUT FROM HIS BROTHERS AND SISTERS AT A YOUNG AGE...
SOME MAY SAY AS A TRUE COMEDIAN, OTHERS MAY SAY ORNERY. EITHER WAY, CONAN HAD A KNACK FOR COMEDY!
CONAN IDOLIZED THE TV COMEDY GODS OF HIS GENERATION LIKE SID CAESAR, THE MARX BROTHERS AND JOHNNY CARSON. WELL, SOME WERE BEFORE HIS TIME... BUT STILL. IDOLS NONETHELESS.

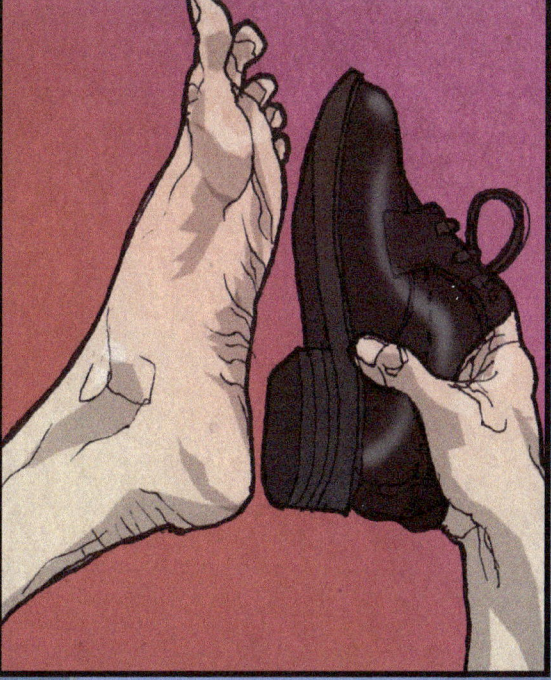

It wasn't until he saw the film *Yankee Doodle Dandy* that Conan was convinced of his fate to be an entertainer. So, naturally, he took tap dancing lessons.

So he didn't become the next James Cagney. So what? He did learn some valuable stage lessons.

Lessons that would come in handy much sooner than he thought.

A quick growth spurt in junior high school cut Conan's tap career short after just a few years. He put dance behind him (for a time) and became devoted to developing the charm and wit that would eventually make him a household name, just like his idols.

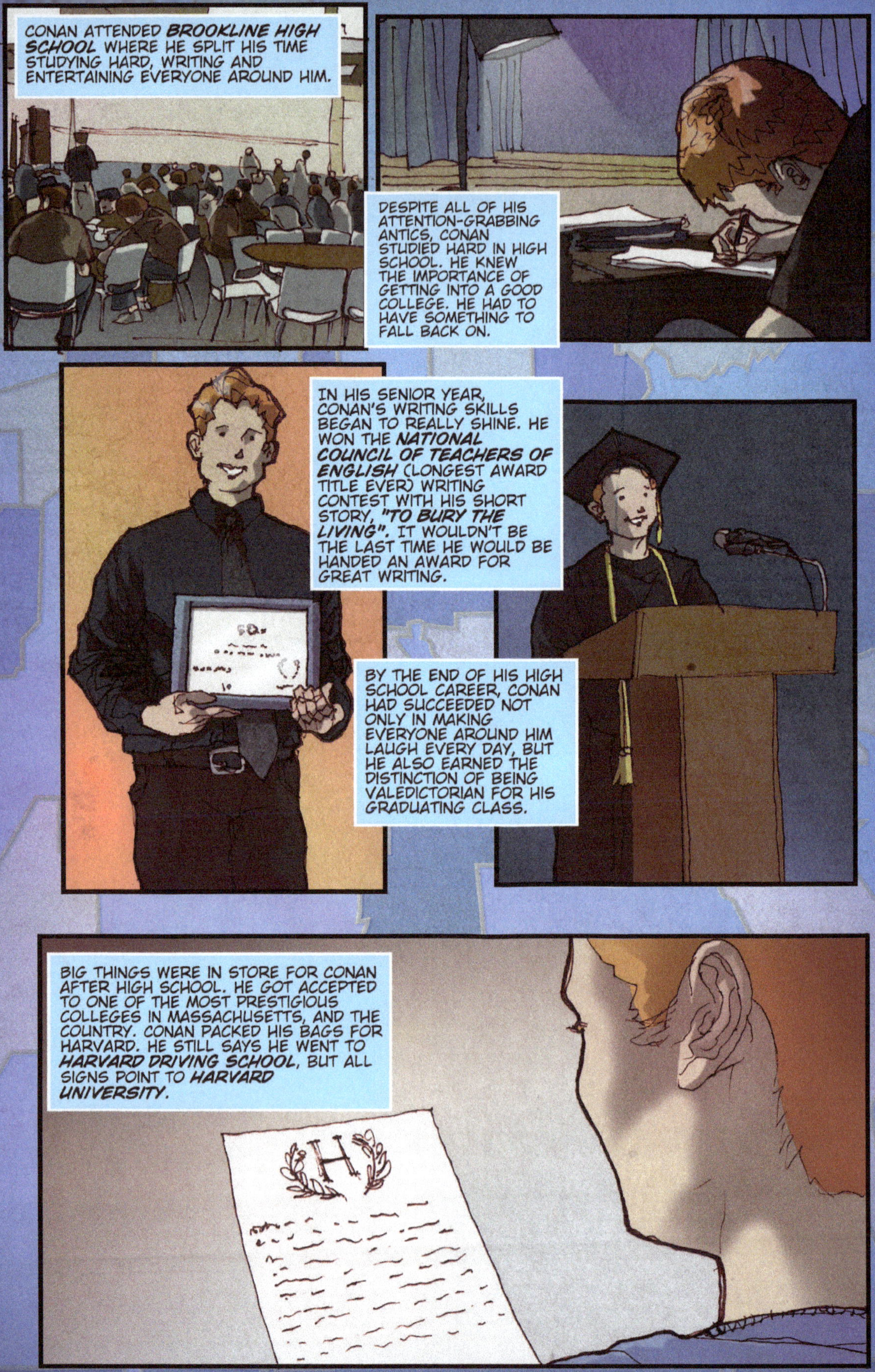
CONAN ATTENDED **BROOKLINE HIGH SCHOOL** WHERE HE SPLIT HIS TIME STUDYING HARD, WRITING AND ENTERTAINING EVERYONE AROUND HIM.
DESPITE ALL OF HIS ATTENTION-GRABBING ANTICS, CONAN STUDIED HARD IN HIGH SCHOOL. HE KNEW THE IMPORTANCE OF GETTING INTO A GOOD COLLEGE. HE HAD TO HAVE SOMETHING TO FALL BACK ON.
IN HIS SENIOR YEAR, CONAN'S WRITING SKILLS BEGAN TO REALLY SHINE. HE WON THE **NATIONAL COUNCIL OF TEACHERS OF ENGLISH** (LONGEST AWARD TITLE EVER) WRITING CONTEST WITH HIS SHORT STORY, **"TO BURY THE LIVING"**. IT WOULDN'T BE THE LAST TIME HE WOULD BE HANDED AN AWARD FOR GREAT WRITING.
BY THE END OF HIS HIGH SCHOOL CAREER, CONAN HAD SUCCEEDED NOT ONLY IN MAKING EVERYONE AROUND HIM LAUGH EVERY DAY, BUT HE ALSO EARNED THE DISTINCTION OF BEING VALEDICTORIAN FOR HIS GRADUATING CLASS.
BIG THINGS WERE IN STORE FOR CONAN AFTER HIGH SCHOOL. HE GOT ACCEPTED TO ONE OF THE MOST PRESTIGIOUS COLLEGES IN MASSACHUSETTS, AND THE COUNTRY. CONAN PACKED HIS BAGS FOR HARVARD. HE STILL SAYS HE WENT TO **HARVARD DRIVING SCHOOL**, BUT ALL SIGNS POINT TO **HARVARD UNIVERSITY**.
H

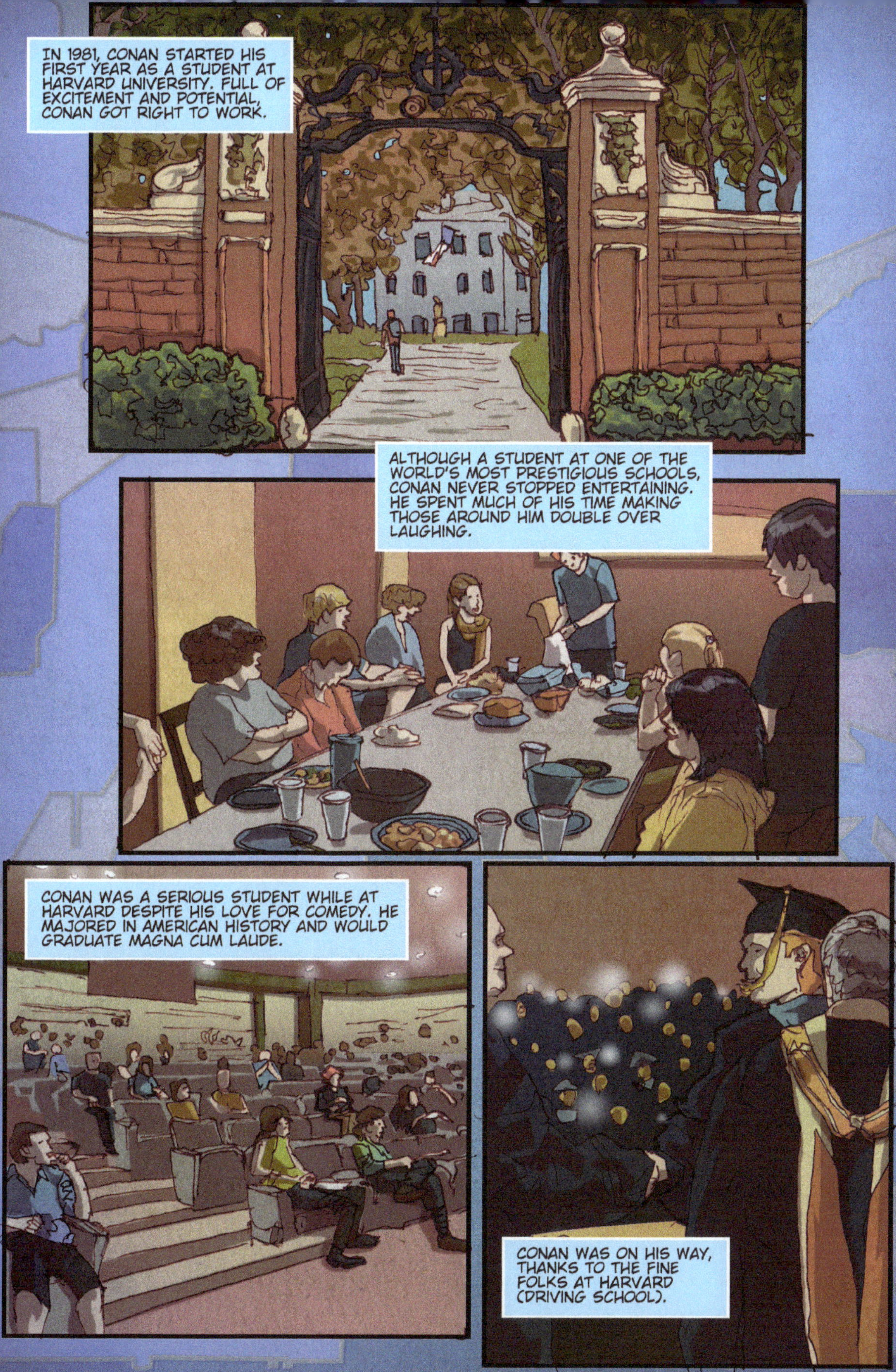
IN 1981, CONAN STARTED HIS FIRST YEAR AS A STUDENT AT HARVARD UNIVERSITY. FULL OF EXCITEMENT AND POTENTIAL, CONAN GOT RIGHT TO WORK.
ALTHOUGH A STUDENT AT ONE OF THE WORLD'S MOST PRESTIGIOUS SCHOOLS, CONAN NEVER STOPPED ENTERTAINING. HE SPENT MUCH OF HIS TIME MAKING THOSE AROUND HIM DOUBLE OVER LAUGHING.
CONAN WAS A SERIOUS STUDENT WHILE AT HARVARD DESPITE HIS LOVE FOR COMEDY. HE MAJORED IN AMERICAN HISTORY AND WOULD GRADUATE MAGNA CUM LAUDE.
CONAN WAS ON HIS WAY, THANKS TO THE FINE FOLKS AT HARVARD (DRIVING SCHOOL).

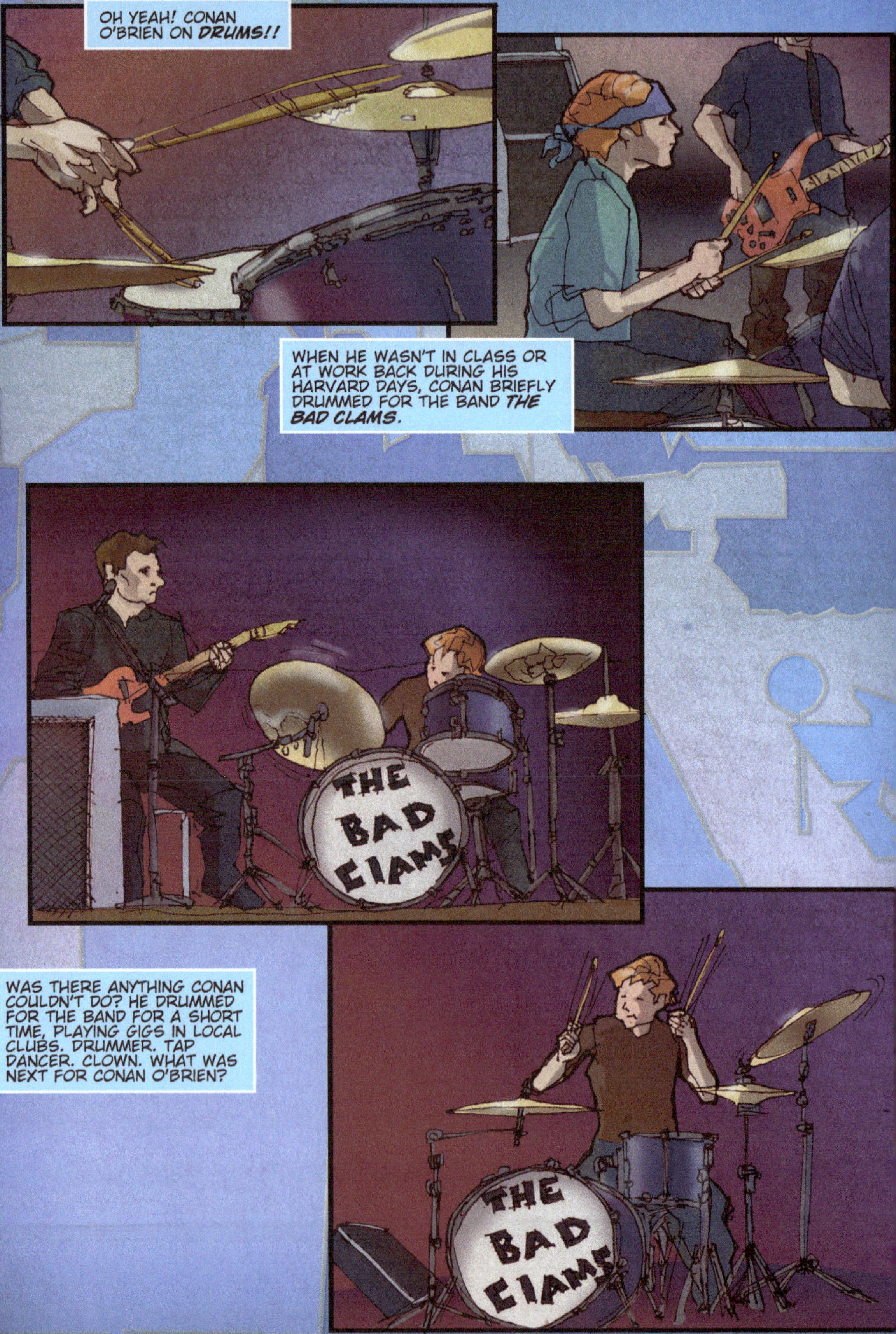
OH YEAH! CONAN O'BRIEN ON DRUMS!!
WHEN HE WASN'T IN CLASS OR AT WORK BACK DURING HIS HARVARD DAYS, CONAN BRIEFLY DRUMMED FOR THE BAND THE BAD CLAMS.
THE BAD CLAMS
WAS THERE ANYTHING CONAN COULDN'T DO? HE DRUMMED FOR THE BAND FOR A SHORT TIME, PLAYING GIGS IN LOCAL CLUBS. DRUMMER. TAP DANCER. CLOWN. WHAT WAS NEXT FOR CONAN O'BRIEN?
THE BAD CLAMS

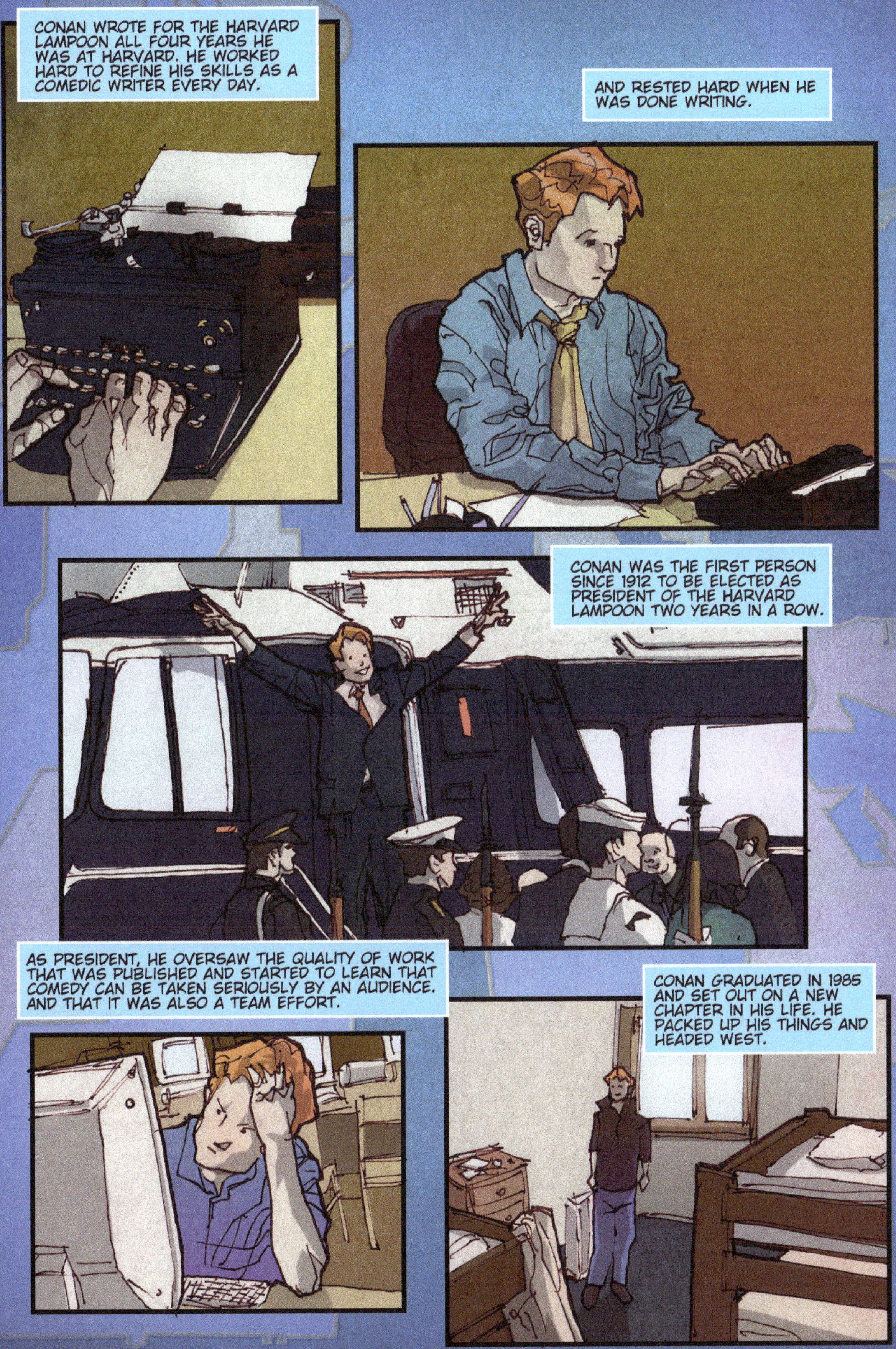
CONAN WROTE FOR THE HARVARD LAMPOON ALL FOUR YEARS HE WAS AT HARVARD. HE WORKED HARD TO REFINE HIS SKILLS AS A COMEDIC WRITER EVERY DAY.
AND RESTED HARD WHEN HE WAS DONE WRITING.
CONAN WAS THE FIRST PERSON SINCE 1912 TO BE ELECTED AS PRESIDENT OF THE HARVARD LAMPOON TWO YEARS IN A ROW.
AS PRESIDENT, HE OVERSAW THE QUALITY OF WORK THAT WAS PUBLISHED AND STARTED TO LEARN THAT COMEDY CAN BE TAKEN SERIOUSLY BY AN AUDIENCE. AND THAT IT WAS ALSO A TEAM EFFORT.
CONAN GRADUATED IN 1985 AND SET OUT ON A NEW CHAPTER IN HIS LIFE. HE PACKED UP HIS THINGS AND HEADED WEST.

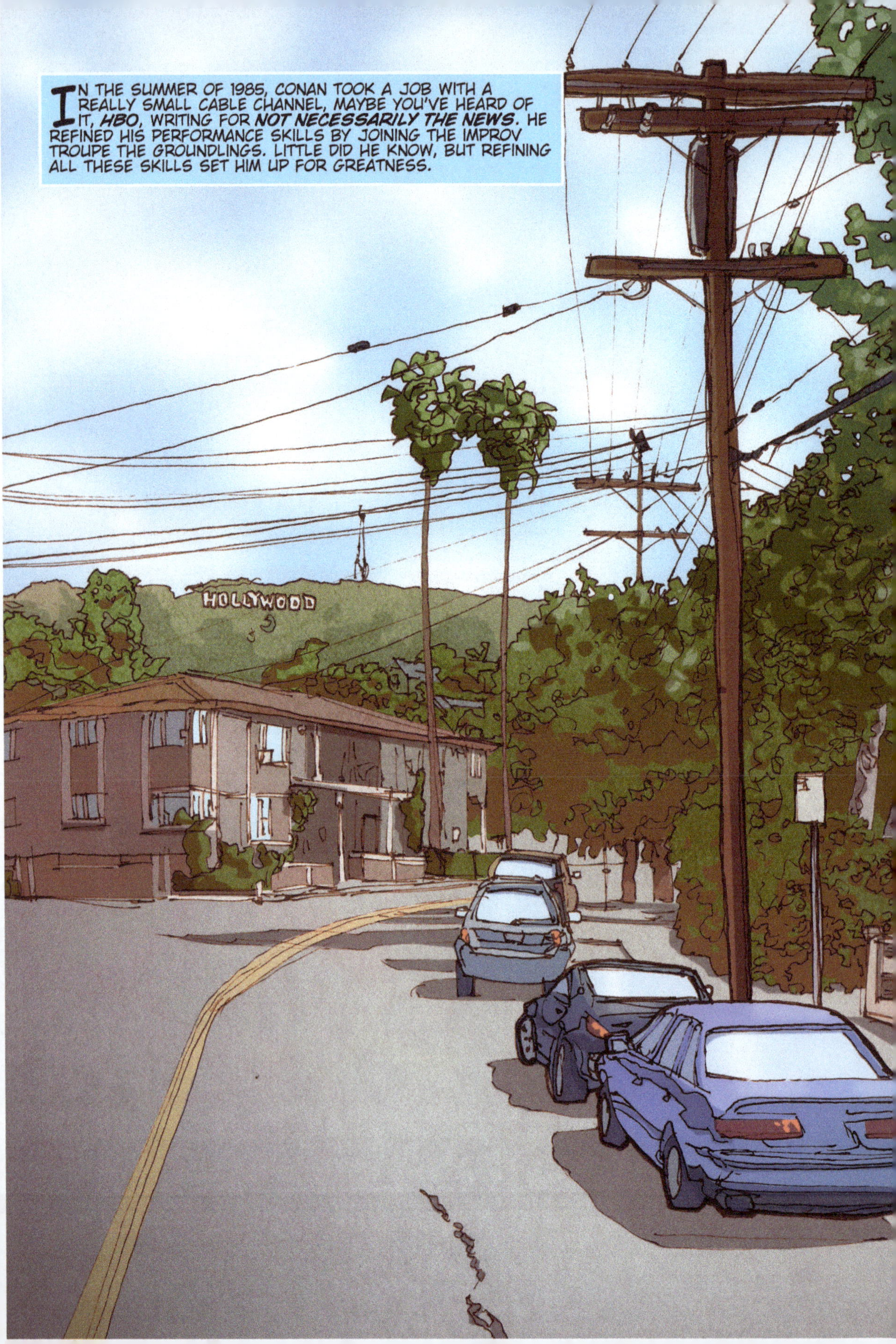
IN THE SUMMER OF 1985, CONAN TOOK A JOB WITH A REALLY SMALL CABLE CHANNEL, MAYBE YOU'VE HEARD OF IT, HBO, WRITING FOR NOT NECESSARILY THE NEWS. HE REFINED HIS PERFORMANCE SKILLS BY JOINING THE IMPROV TROUPE THE GROUNDLINGS. LITTLE DID HE KNOW, BUT REFINING ALL THESE SKILLS SET HIM UP FOR GREATNESS.
HOLLYWOOD

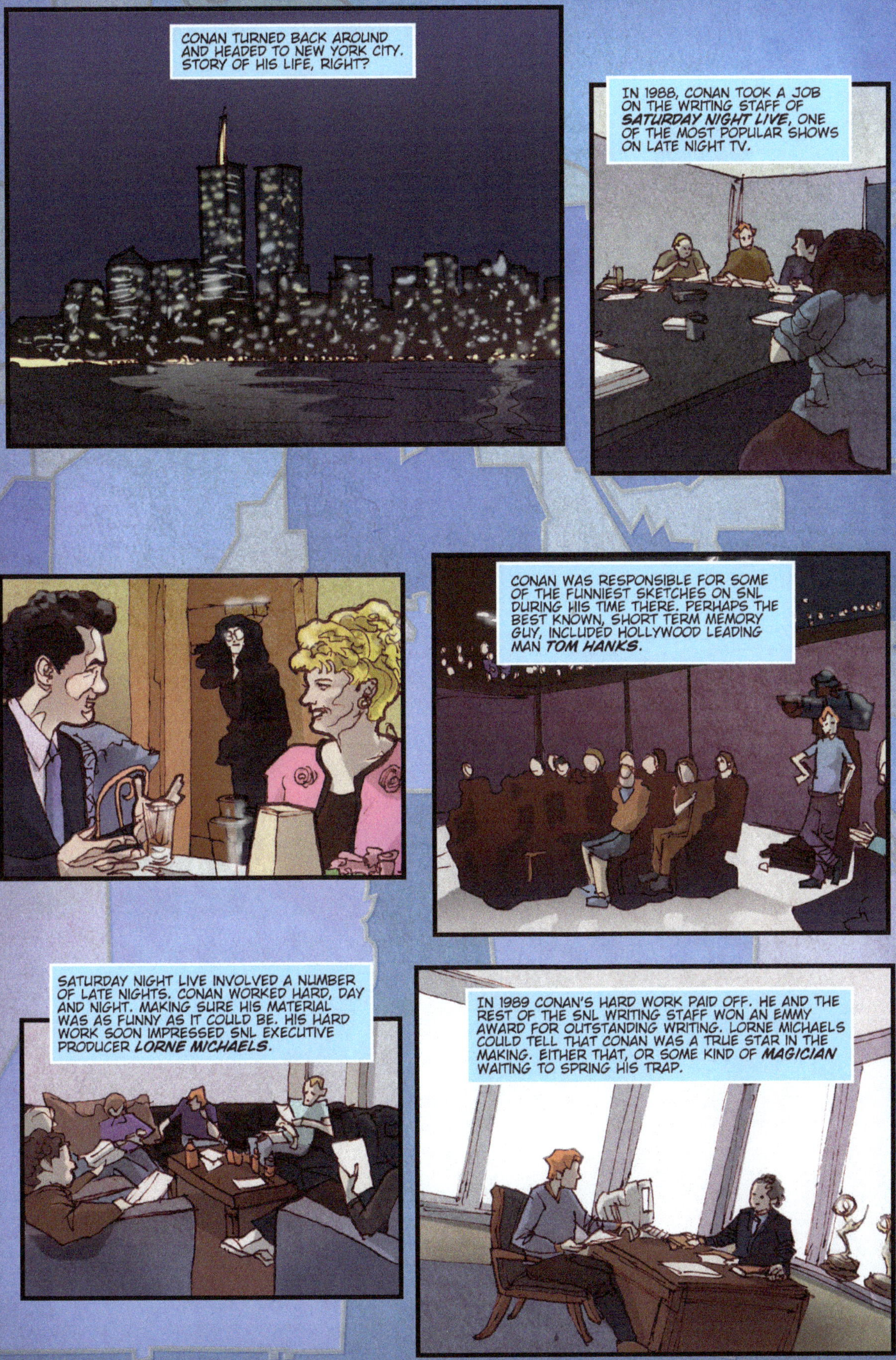
CONAN TURNED BACK AROUND AND HEADED TO NEW YORK CITY. STORY OF HIS LIFE, RIGHT?
IN 1988, CONAN TOOK A JOB ON THE WRITING STAFF OF *SATURDAY NIGHT LIVE*, ONE OF THE MOST POPULAR SHOWS ON LATE NIGHT TV.
CONAN WAS RESPONSIBLE FOR SOME OF THE FUNNIEST SKETCHES ON SNL DURING HIS TIME THERE. PERHAPS THE BEST KNOWN, SHORT TERM MEMORY GUY, INCLUDED HOLLYWOOD LEADING MAN *TOM HANKS*.
SATURDAY NIGHT LIVE INVOLVED A NUMBER OF LATE NIGHTS. CONAN WORKED HARD, DAY AND NIGHT. MAKING SURE HIS MATERIAL WAS AS FUNNY AS IT COULD BE. HIS HARD WORK SOON IMPRESSED SNL EXECUTIVE PRODUCER *LORNE MICHAELS*.
IN 1989 CONAN'S HARD WORK PAID OFF. HE AND THE REST OF THE SNL WRITING STAFF WON AN EMMY AWARD FOR OUTSTANDING WRITING. LORNE MICHAELS COULD TELL THAT CONAN WAS A TRUE STAR IN THE MAKING. EITHER THAT, OR SOME KIND OF *MAGICIAN* WAITING TO SPRING HIS TRAP.

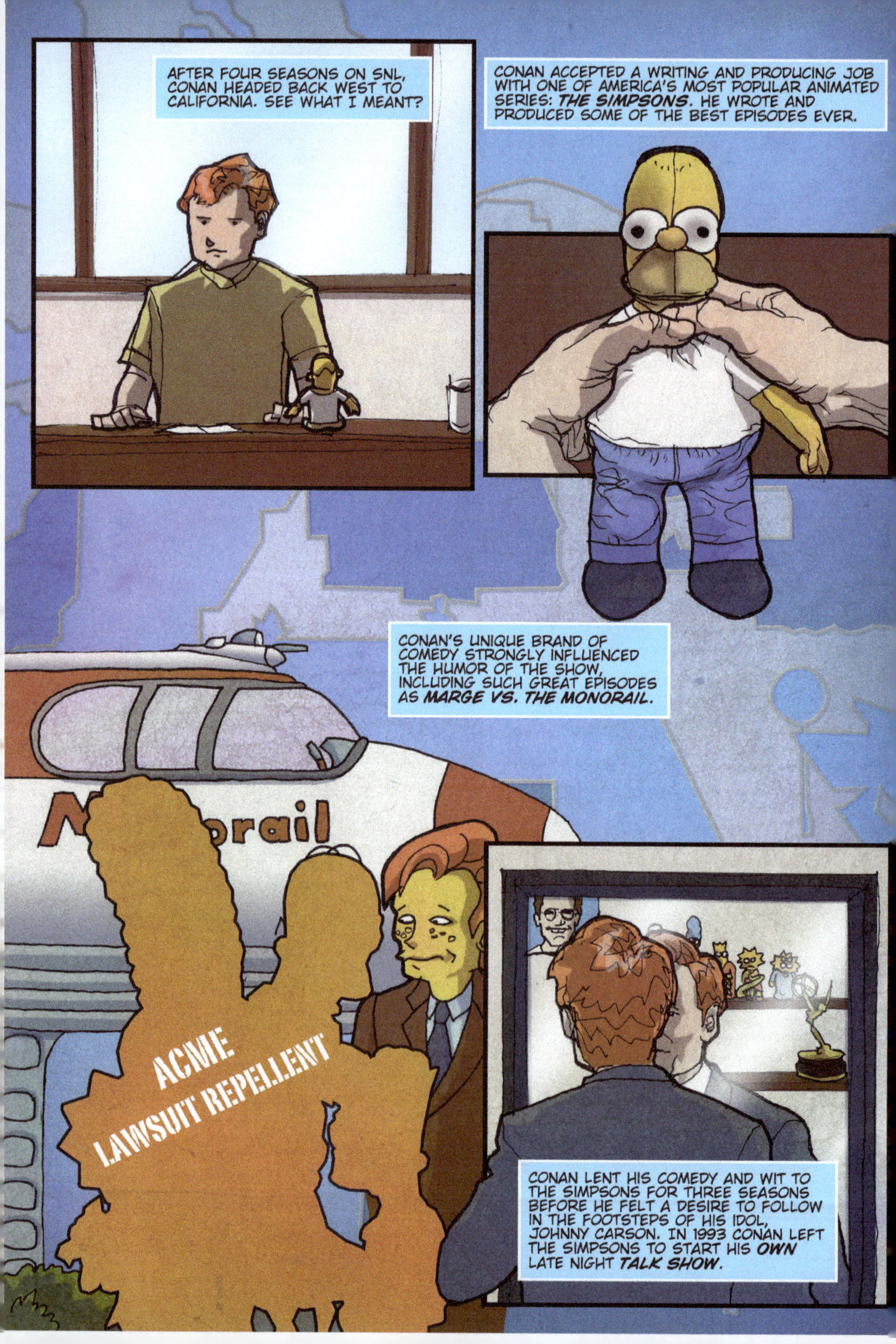
AFTER FOUR SEASONS ON SNL, CONAN HEADED BACK WEST TO CALIFORNIA. SEE WHAT I MEANT?
CONAN ACCEPTED A WRITING AND PRODUCING JOB WITH ONE OF AMERICA'S MOST POPULAR ANIMATED SERIES: THE SIMPSONS. HE WROTE AND PRODUCED SOME OF THE BEST EPISODES EVER.
CONAN'S UNIQUE BRAND OF COMEDY STRONGLY INFLUENCED THE HUMOR OF THE SHOW, INCLUDING SUCH GREAT EPISODES AS MARGE VS. THE MONORAIL.
ACME
LAWSUIT REPELLENT
CONAN LENT HIS COMEDY AND WIT TO THE SIMPSONS FOR THREE SEASONS BEFORE HE FELT A DESIRE TO FOLLOW IN THE FOOTSTEPS OF HIS IDOL, JOHNNY CARSON. IN 1993 CONAN LEFT THE SIMPSONS TO START HIS OWN LATE NIGHT TALK SHOW.

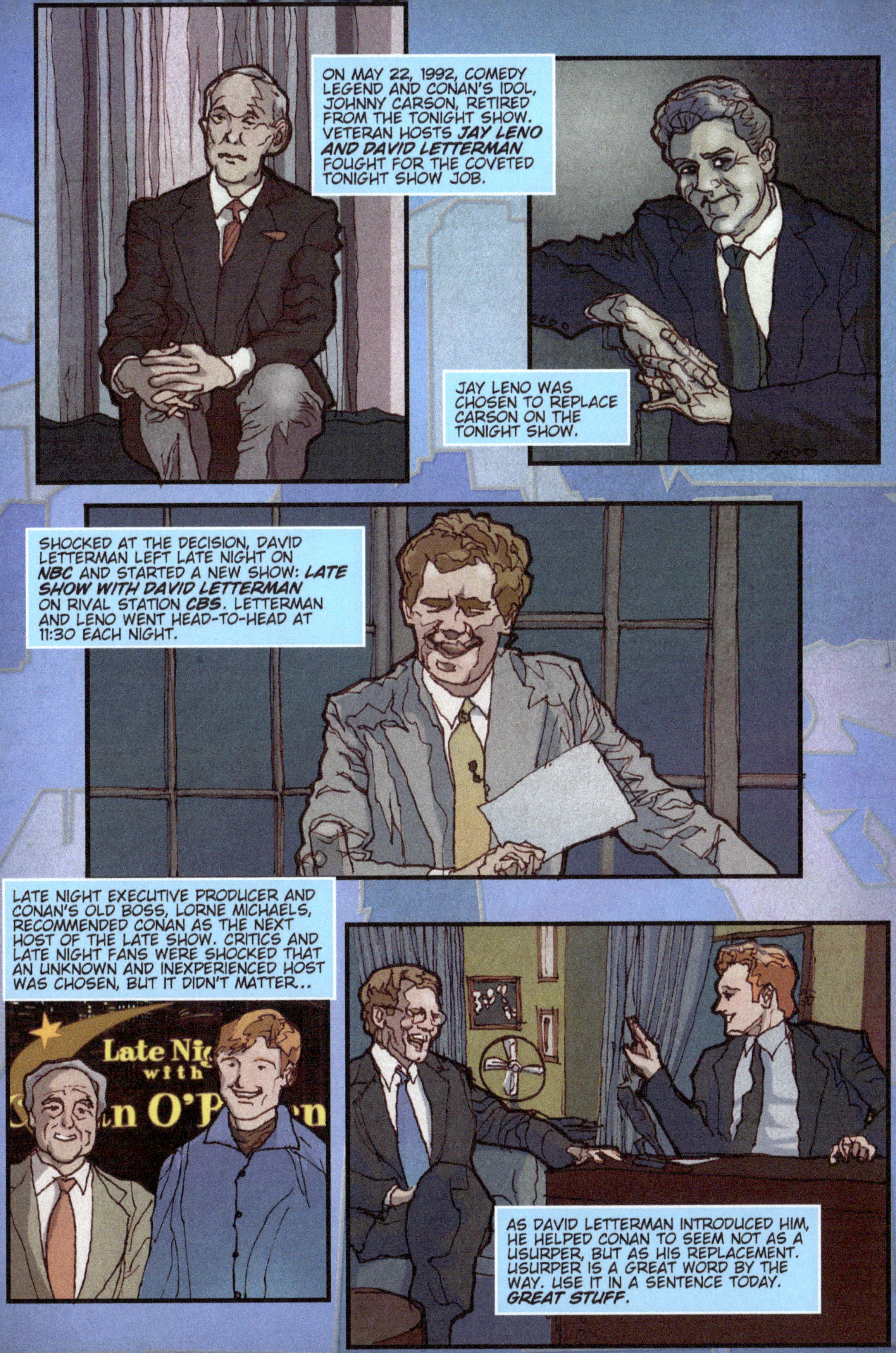
ON MAY 22, 1992, COMEDY LEGEND AND CONAN'S IDOL, JOHNNY CARSON, RETIRED FROM THE TONIGHT SHOW. VETERAN HOSTS JAY LENO AND DAVID LETTERMAN FOUGHT FOR THE COVETED TONIGHT SHOW JOB.
JAY LENO WAS CHOSEN TO REPLACE CARSON ON THE TONIGHT SHOW.
SHOCKED AT THE DECISION, DAVID LETTERMAN LEFT LATE NIGHT ON NBC AND STARTED A NEW SHOW: LATE SHOW WITH DAVID LETTERMAN ON RIVAL STATION CBS. LETTERMAN AND LENO WENT HEAD-TO-HEAD AT 11:30 EACH NIGHT.
LATE NIGHT EXECUTIVE PRODUCER AND CONAN'S OLD BOSS, LORNE MICHAELS, RECOMMENDED CONAN AS THE NEXT HOST OF THE LATE SHOW. CRITICS AND LATE NIGHT FANS WERE SHOCKED THAT AN UNKNOWN AND INEXPERIENCED HOST WAS CHOSEN, BUT IT DIDN'T MATTER...
AS DAVID LETTERMAN INTRODUCED HIM, HE HELPED CONAN TO SEEM NOT AS A USURPER, BUT AS HIS REPLACEMENT. USURPER IS A GREAT WORD BY THE WAY. USE IT IN A SENTENCE TODAY. GREAT STUFF.

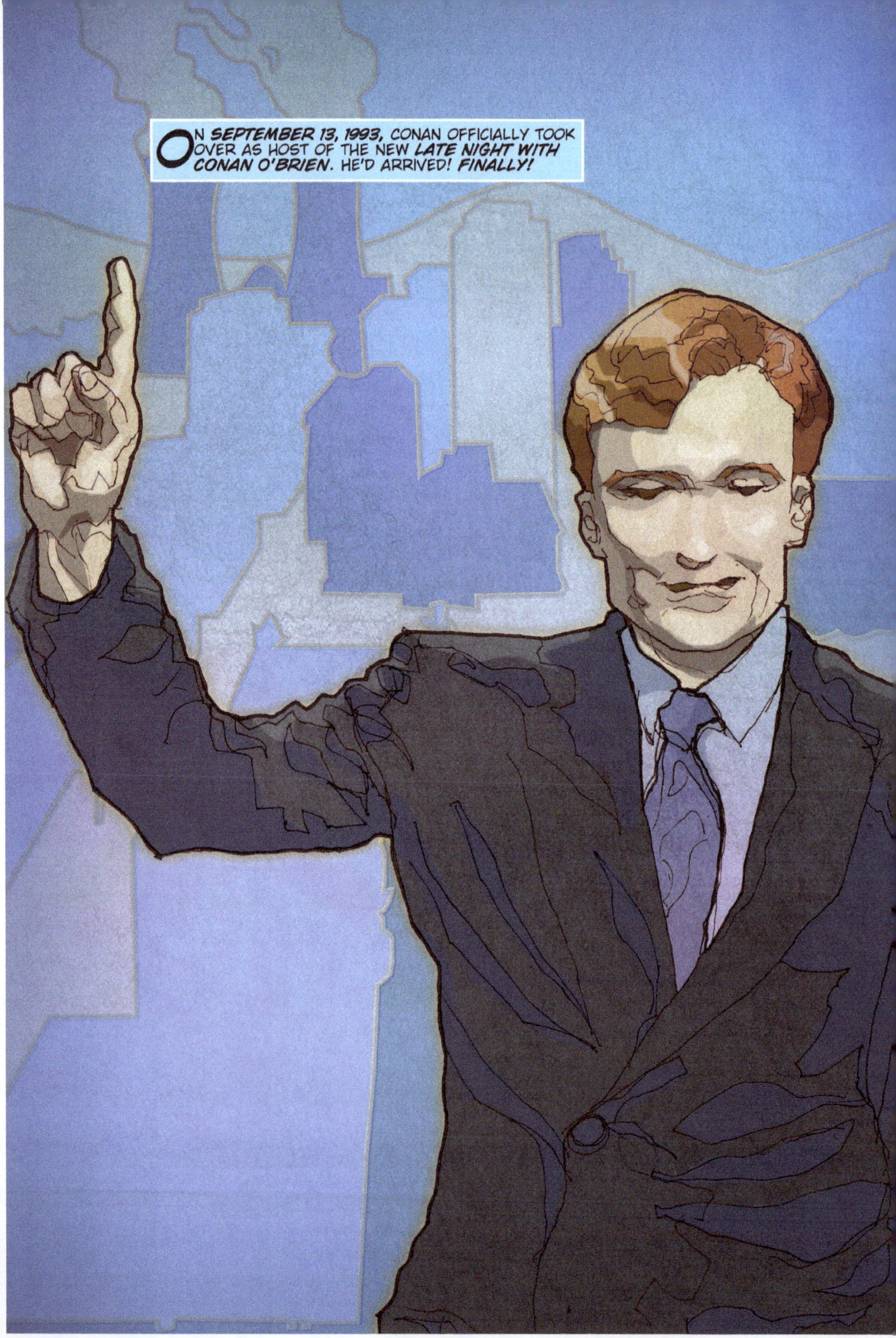
ON SEPTEMBER 13, 1993, CONAN OFFICIALLY TOOK OVER AS HOST OF THE NEW LATE NIGHT WITH CONAN O'BRIEN. HE'D ARRIVED! FINALLY!

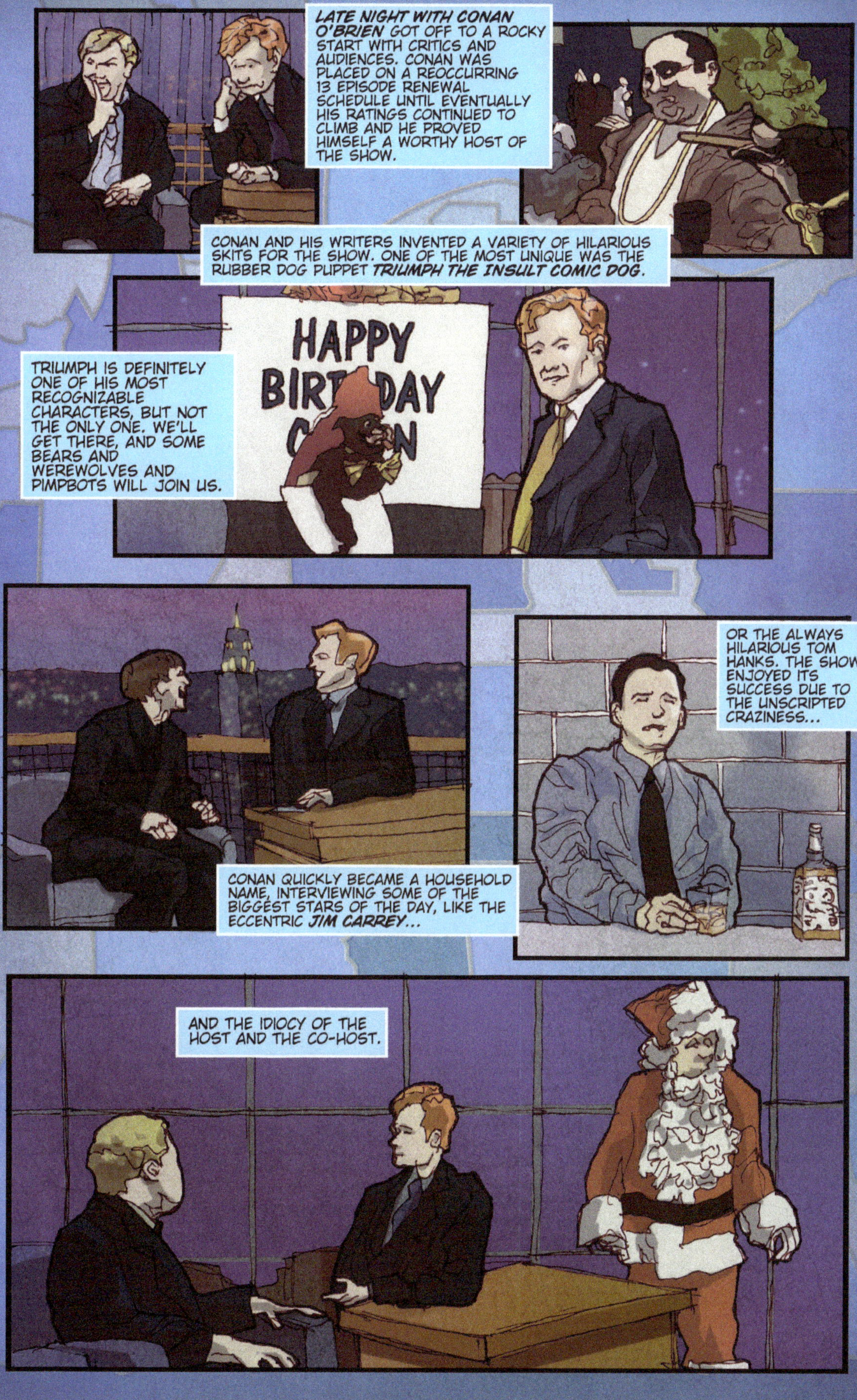
LATE NIGHT WITH CONAN O'BRIEN GOT OFF TO A ROCKY START WITH CRITICS AND AUDIENCES. CONAN WAS PLACED ON A REOCCURRING 13 EPISODE RENEWAL SCHEDULE UNTIL EVENTUALLY HIS RATINGS CONTINUED TO CLIMB AND HE PROVED HIMSELF A WORTHY HOST OF THE SHOW.
CONAN AND HIS WRITERS INVENTED A VARIETY OF HILARIOUS SKITS FOR THE SHOW. ONE OF THE MOST UNIQUE WAS THE RUBBER DOG PUPPET ***TRIUMPH THE INSULT COMIC DOG***.
HAPPY BIRT DAY
TRIUMPH IS DEFINITELY ONE OF HIS MOST RECOGNIZABLE CHARACTERS, BUT NOT THE ONLY ONE. WE'LL GET THERE, AND SOME BEARS AND WEREWOLVES AND PIMPBOTS WILL JOIN US.
CONAN QUICKLY BECAME A HOUSEHOLD NAME, INTERVIEWING SOME OF THE BIGGEST STARS OF THE DAY, LIKE THE ECCENTRIC ***JIM CARREY***...
OR THE ALWAYS HILARIOUS TOM HANKS. THE SHOW ENJOYED ITS SUCCESS DUE TO THE UNSCRIPTED CRAZINESS...
AND THE IDIOCY OF THE HOST AND THE CO-HOST.

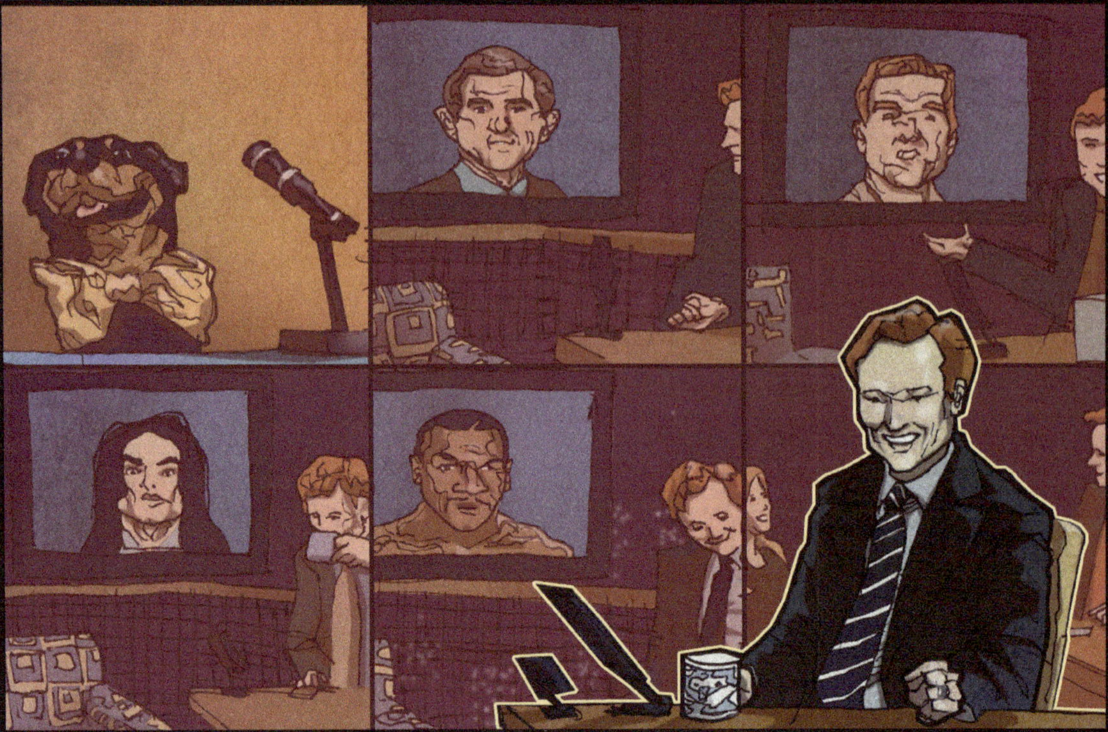

FOR YEARS, THIS BRAND OF IDIOCY PLAYED TO A CROWD OF MILLIONS. YOUNG AND OLD, CONAN FOUND HIS AUDIENCE. HIS COMEDY BLOSSOMED FROM SMALL BITS ABOUT HIM AND ANDY TO HUGE MOMENTS INVOLVING EXPLOSIONS AND A DRIVING DRUM SET. AND AS IT BLOSSOMED, MORE PEOPLE WOULD TAKE NOTICE, AND MORE WOULD WANT TO BE IN ON THE JOKE...

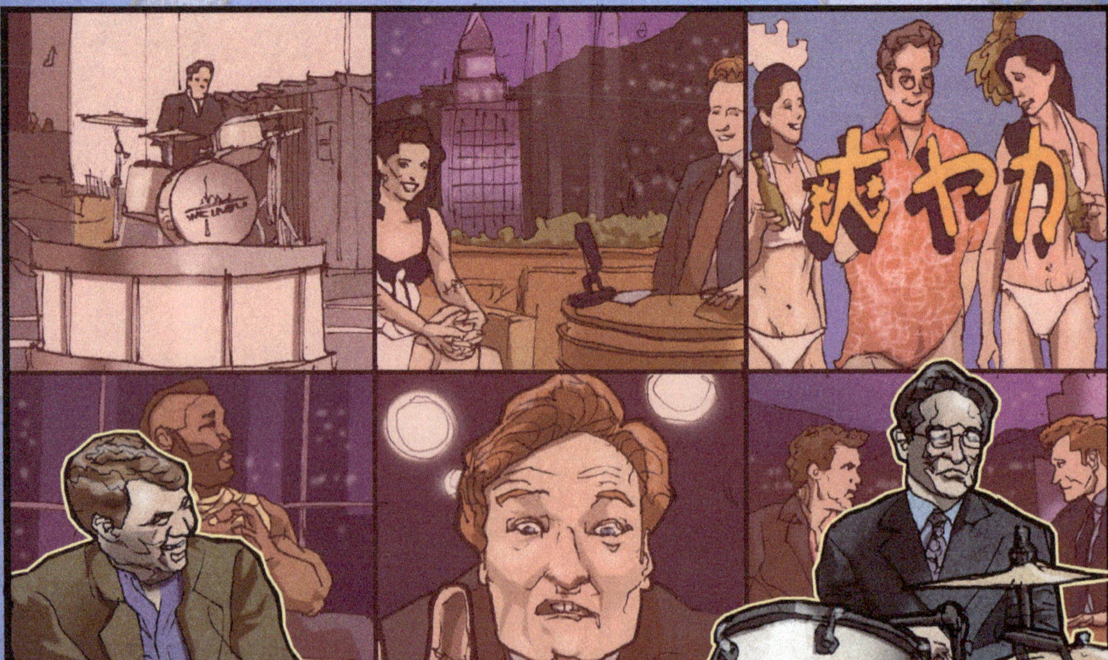

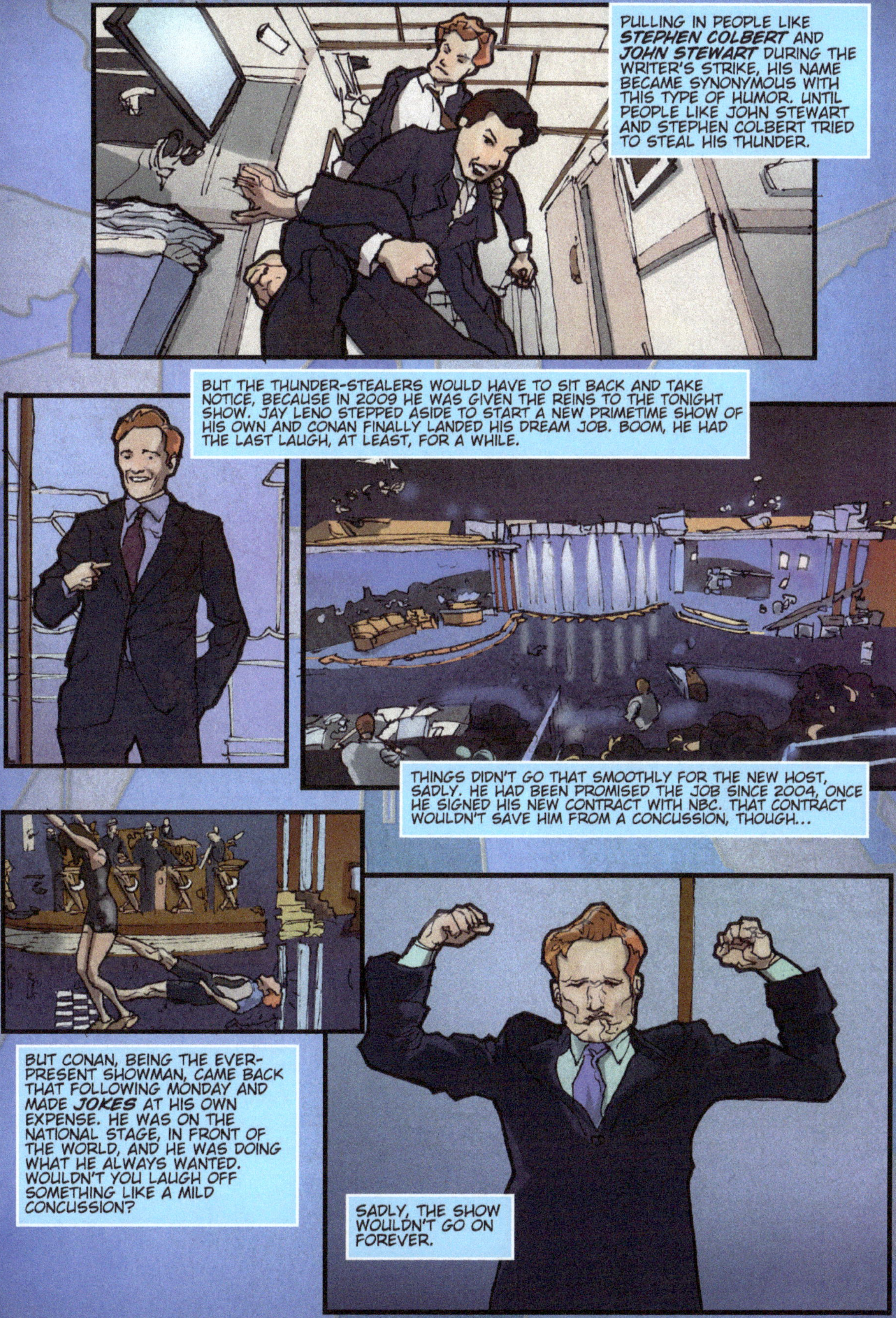

PULLING IN PEOPLE LIKE STEPHEN COLBERT AND JOHN STEWART DURING THE WRITER'S STRIKE, HIS NAME BECAME SYNONYMOUS WITH THIS TYPE OF HUMOR. UNTIL PEOPLE LIKE JOHN STEWART AND STEPHEN COLBERT TRIED TO STEAL HIS THUNDER.
BUT THE THUNDER-STEALERS WOULD HAVE TO SIT BACK AND TAKE NOTICE, BECAUSE IN 2009 HE WAS GIVEN THE REINS TO THE TONIGHT SHOW. JAY LENO STEPPED ASIDE TO START A NEW PRIMETIME SHOW OF HIS OWN AND CONAN FINALLY LANDED HIS DREAM JOB. BOOM, HE HAD THE LAST LAUGH, AT LEAST, FOR A WHILE.
THINGS DIDN'T GO THAT SMOOTHLY FOR THE NEW HOST, SADLY. HE HAD BEEN PROMISED THE JOB SINCE 2004, ONCE HE SIGNED HIS NEW CONTRACT WITH NBC. THAT CONTRACT WOULDN'T SAVE HIM FROM A CONCUSSION, THOUGH...
BUT CONAN, BEING THE EVER-PRESENT SHOWMAN, CAME BACK THAT FOLLOWING MONDAY AND MADE JOKES AT HIS OWN EXPENSE. HE WAS ON THE NATIONAL STAGE, IN FRONT OF THE WORLD, AND HE WAS DOING WHAT HE ALWAYS WANTED. WOULDN'T YOU LAUGH OFF SOMETHING LIKE A MILD CONCUSSION?
SADLY, THE SHOW WOULDN'T GO ON FOREVER.

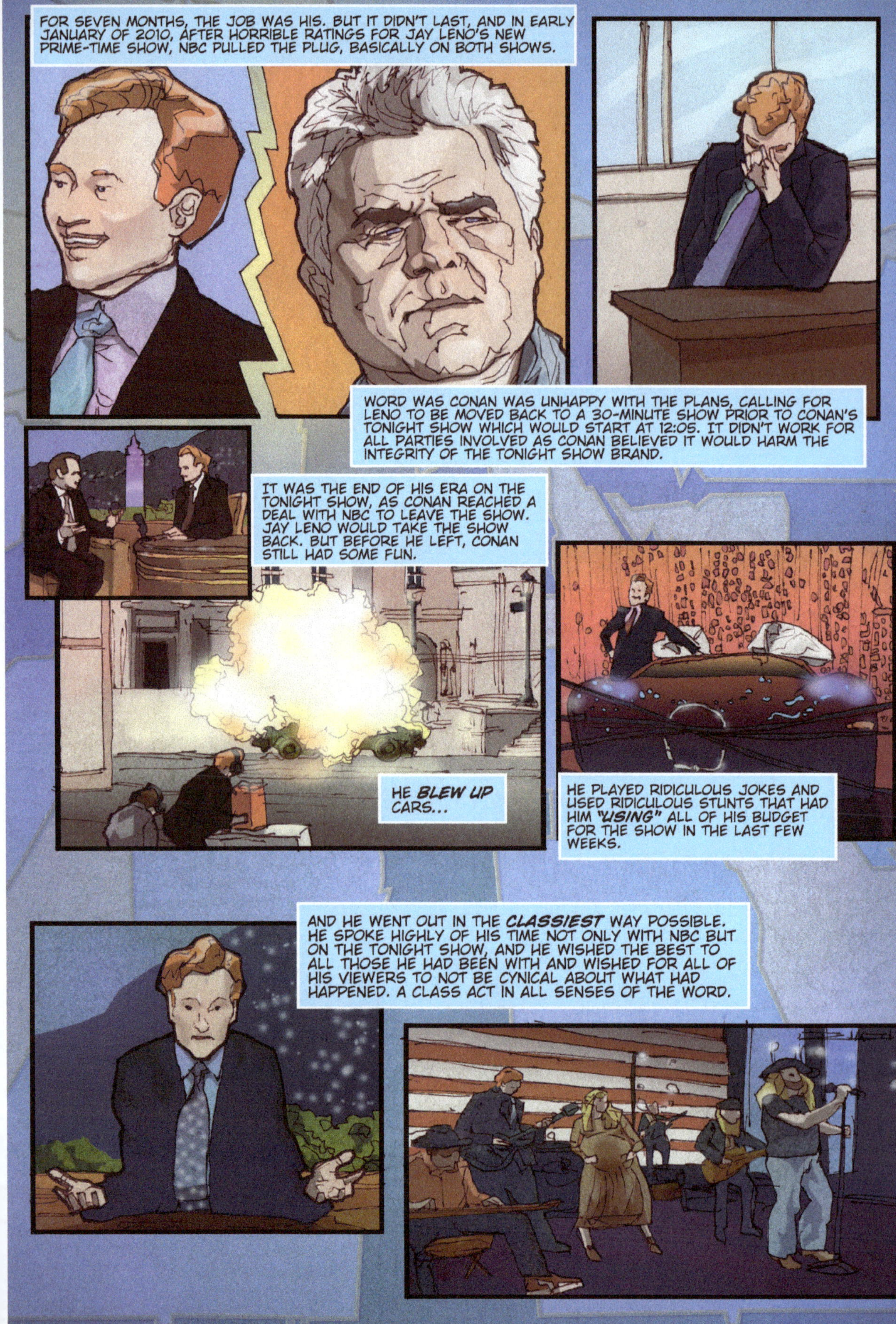
FOR SEVEN MONTHS, THE JOB WAS HIS. BUT IT DIDN'T LAST, AND IN EARLY JANUARY OF 2010, AFTER HORRIBLE RATINGS FOR JAY LENO'S NEW PRIME-TIME SHOW, NBC PULLED THE PLUG, BASICALLY ON BOTH SHOWS.
WORD WAS CONAN WAS UNHAPPY WITH THE PLANS, CALLING FOR LENO TO BE MOVED BACK TO A 30-MINUTE SHOW PRIOR TO CONAN'S TONIGHT SHOW WHICH WOULD START AT 12:05. IT DIDN'T WORK FOR ALL PARTIES INVOLVED AS CONAN BELIEVED IT WOULD HARM THE INTEGRITY OF THE TONIGHT SHOW BRAND.
IT WAS THE END OF HIS ERA ON THE TONIGHT SHOW, AS CONAN REACHED A DEAL WITH NBC TO LEAVE THE SHOW. JAY LENO WOULD TAKE THE SHOW BACK. BUT BEFORE HE LEFT, CONAN STILL HAD SOME FUN.
HE **BLEW UP** CARS...
HE PLAYED RIDICULOUS JOKES AND USED RIDICULOUS STUNTS THAT HAD HIM **"USING"** ALL OF HIS BUDGET FOR THE SHOW IN THE LAST FEW WEEKS.
AND HE WENT OUT IN THE **CLASSIEST** WAY POSSIBLE. HE SPOKE HIGHLY OF HIS TIME NOT ONLY WITH NBC BUT ON THE TONIGHT SHOW, AND HE WISHED THE BEST TO ALL THOSE HE HAD BEEN WITH AND WISHED FOR ALL OF HIS VIEWERS TO NOT BE CYNICAL ABOUT WHAT HAD HAPPENED. A CLASS ACT IN ALL SENSES OF THE WORD.

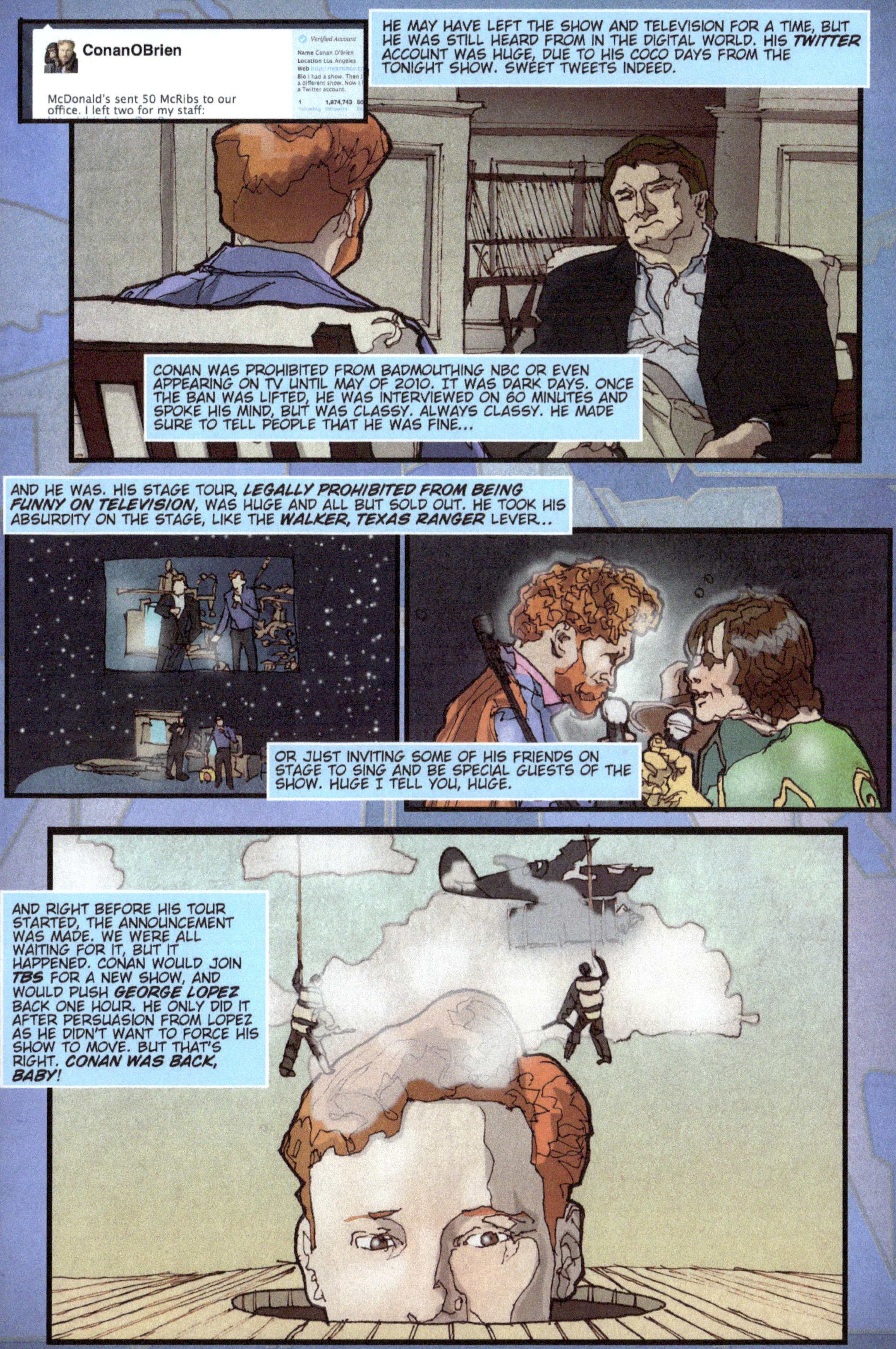
ConanOBrien
Verified Account
McDonald's sent 50 McRibs to our office. I left two for my staff:
HE MAY HAVE LEFT THE SHOW AND TELEVISION FOR A TIME, BUT HE WAS STILL HEARD FROM IN THE DIGITAL WORLD. HIS *TWITTER* ACCOUNT WAS HUGE, DUE TO HIS COCO DAYS FROM THE TONIGHT SHOW. SWEET TWEETS INDEED.
CONAN WAS PROHIBITED FROM BADMOUTHING NBC OR EVEN APPEARING ON TV UNTIL MAY OF 2010. IT WAS DARK DAYS. ONCE THE BAN WAS LIFTED, HE WAS INTERVIEWED ON 60 MINUTES AND SPOKE HIS MIND, BUT WAS CLASSY. ALWAYS CLASSY. HE MADE SURE TO TELL PEOPLE THAT HE WAS FINE...
AND HE WAS. HIS STAGE TOUR, ***LEGALLY PROHIBITED FROM BEING FUNNY ON TELEVISION***, WAS HUGE AND ALL BUT SOLD OUT. HE TOOK HIS ABSURDITY ON THE STAGE, LIKE THE ***WALKER, TEXAS RANGER*** LEVER...
OR JUST INVITING SOME OF HIS FRIENDS ON STAGE TO SING AND BE SPECIAL GUESTS OF THE SHOW. HUGE I TELL YOU, HUGE.
AND RIGHT BEFORE HIS TOUR STARTED, THE ANNOUNCEMENT WAS MADE. WE WERE ALL WAITING FOR IT, BUT IT HAPPENED. CONAN WOULD JOIN ***TBS*** FOR A NEW SHOW, AND WOULD PUSH ***GEORGE LOPEZ*** BACK ONE HOUR. HE ONLY DID IT AFTER PERSUASION FROM LOPEZ AS HE DIDN'T WANT TO FORCE HIS SHOW TO MOVE. BUT THAT'S RIGHT. ***CONAN WAS BACK, BABY!***

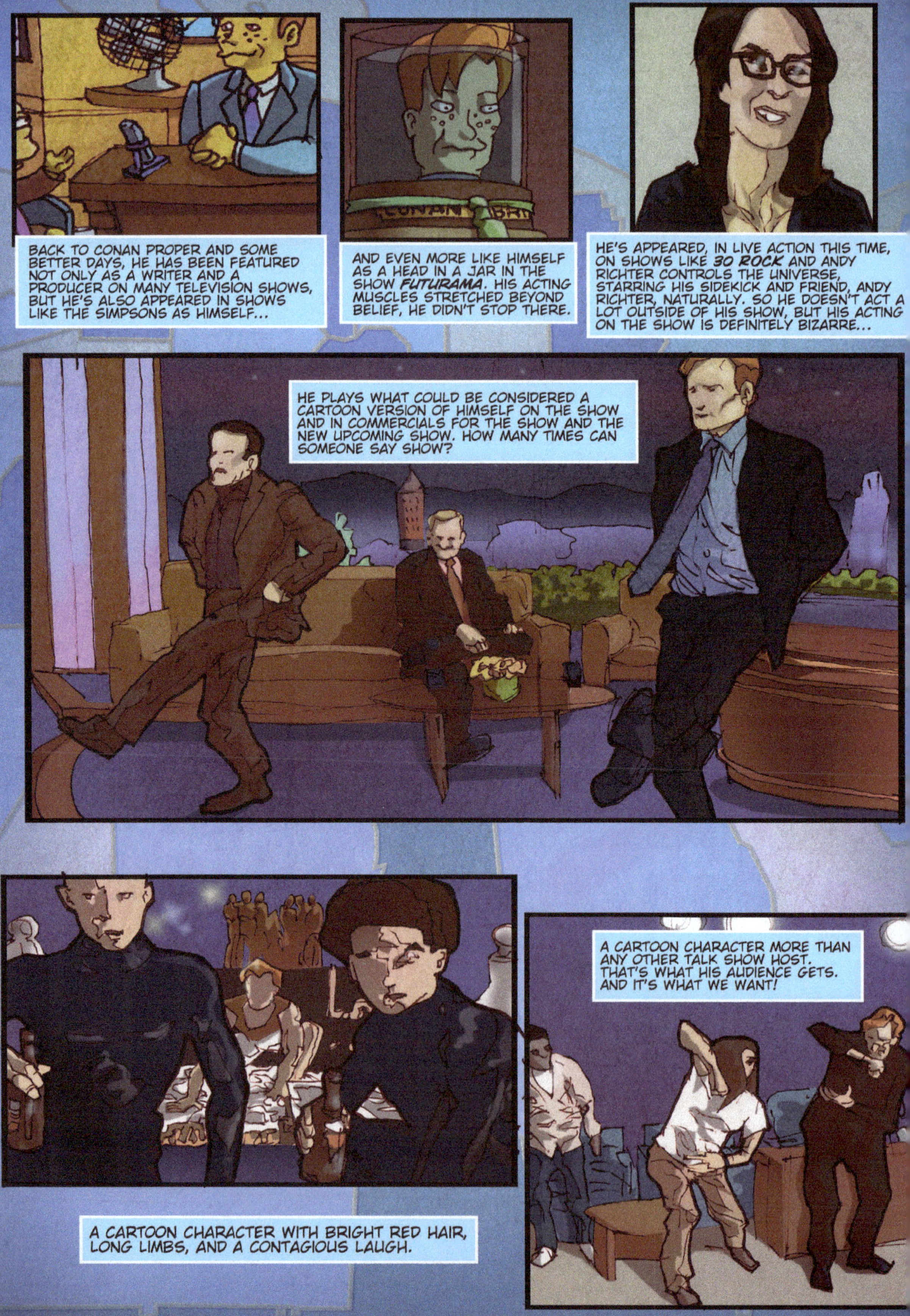
BACK TO CONAN PROPER AND SOME BETTER DAYS, HE HAS BEEN FEATURED NOT ONLY AS A WRITER AND A PRODUCER ON MANY TELEVISION SHOWS, BUT HE'S ALSO APPEARED IN SHOWS LIKE THE SIMPSONS AS HIMSELF...
AND EVEN MORE LIKE HIMSELF AS A HEAD IN A JAR IN THE SHOW *FUTURAMA*. HIS ACTING MUSCLES STRETCHED BEYOND BELIEF, HE DIDN'T STOP THERE.
HE'S APPEARED, IN LIVE ACTION THIS TIME, ON SHOWS LIKE *30 ROCK* AND ANDY RICHTER CONTROLS THE UNIVERSE, STARRING HIS SIDEKICK AND FRIEND, ANDY RICHTER, NATURALLY. SO HE DOESN'T ACT A LOT OUTSIDE OF HIS SHOW, BUT HIS ACTING ON THE SHOW IS DEFINITELY BIZARRE...
HE PLAYS WHAT COULD BE CONSIDERED A CARTOON VERSION OF HIMSELF ON THE SHOW AND IN COMMERCIALS FOR THE SHOW AND THE NEW UPCOMING SHOW. HOW MANY TIMES CAN SOMEONE SAY SHOW?
A CARTOON CHARACTER WITH BRIGHT RED HAIR, LONG LIMBS, AND A CONTAGIOUS LAUGH.
A CARTOON CHARACTER MORE THAN ANY OTHER TALK SHOW HOST. THAT'S WHAT HIS AUDIENCE GETS. AND IT'S WHAT WE WANT!

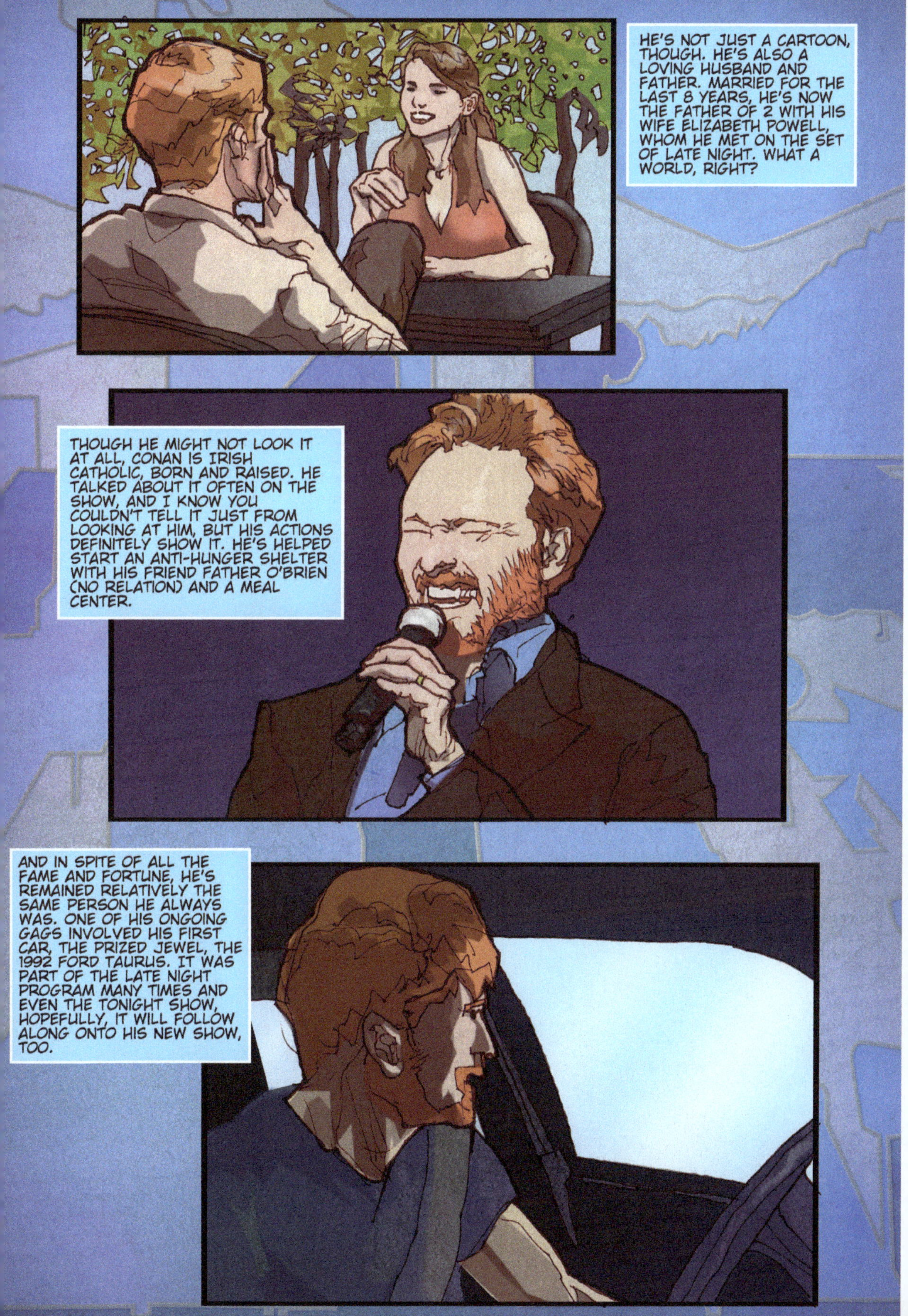
HE'S NOT JUST A CARTOON, THOUGH. HE'S ALSO A LOVING HUSBAND AND FATHER. MARRIED FOR THE LAST 8 YEARS, HE'S NOW THE FATHER OF 2 WITH HIS WIFE ELIZABETH POWELL, WHOM HE MET ON THE SET OF LATE NIGHT. WHAT A WORLD, RIGHT?
THOUGH HE MIGHT NOT LOOK IT AT ALL, CONAN IS IRISH CATHOLIC, BORN AND RAISED. HE TALKED ABOUT IT OFTEN ON THE SHOW, AND I KNOW YOU COULDN'T TELL IT JUST FROM LOOKING AT HIM, BUT HIS ACTIONS DEFINITELY SHOW IT. HE'S HELPED START AN ANTI-HUNGER SHELTER WITH HIS FRIEND FATHER O'BRIEN (NO RELATION) AND A MEAL CENTER.
AND IN SPITE OF ALL THE FAME AND FORTUNE, HE'S REMAINED RELATIVELY THE SAME PERSON HE ALWAYS WAS. ONE OF HIS ONGOING GAGS INVOLVED HIS FIRST CAR, THE PRIZED JEWEL, THE 1992 FORD TAURUS. IT WAS PART OF THE LATE NIGHT PROGRAM MANY TIMES AND EVEN THE TONIGHT SHOW, HOPEFULLY, IT WILL FOLLOW ALONG ONTO HIS NEW SHOW, TOO.

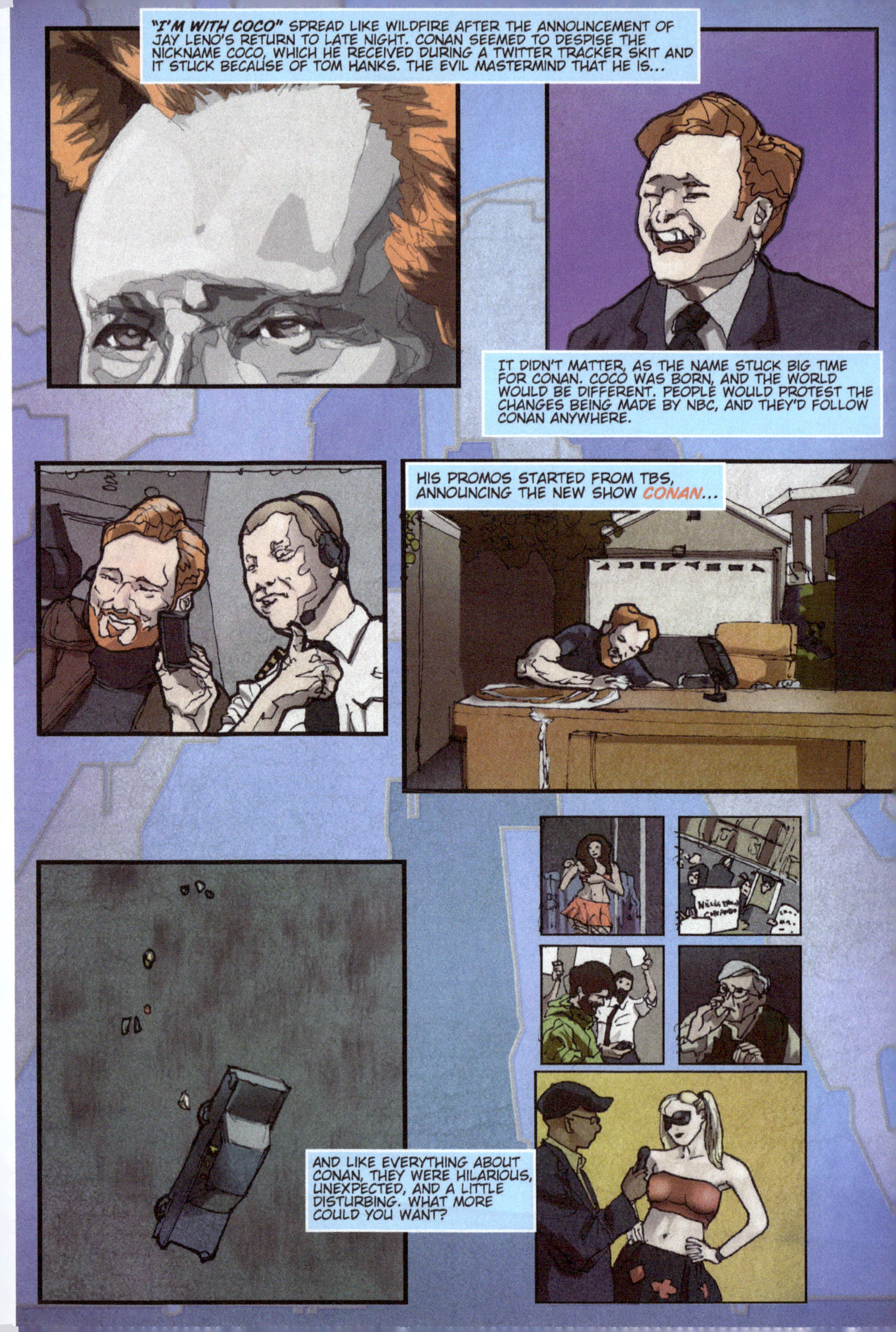
"I'M WITH COCO" SPREAD LIKE WILDFIRE AFTER THE ANNOUNCEMENT OF JAY LENO'S RETURN TO LATE NIGHT. CONAN SEEMED TO DESPISE THE NICKNAME COCO, WHICH HE RECEIVED DURING A TWITTER TRACKER SKIT AND IT STUCK BECAUSE OF TOM HANKS. THE EVIL MASTERMIND THAT HE IS...
IT DIDN'T MATTER, AS THE NAME STUCK BIG TIME FOR CONAN. COCO WAS BORN, AND THE WORLD WOULD BE DIFFERENT. PEOPLE WOULD PROTEST THE CHANGES BEING MADE BY NBC, AND THEY'D FOLLOW CONAN ANYWHERE.
HIS PROMOS STARTED FROM TBS, ANNOUNCING THE NEW SHOW CONAN...
AND LIKE EVERYTHING ABOUT CONAN, THEY WERE HILARIOUS, UNEXPECTED, AND A LITTLE DISTURBING. WHAT MORE COULD YOU WANT?

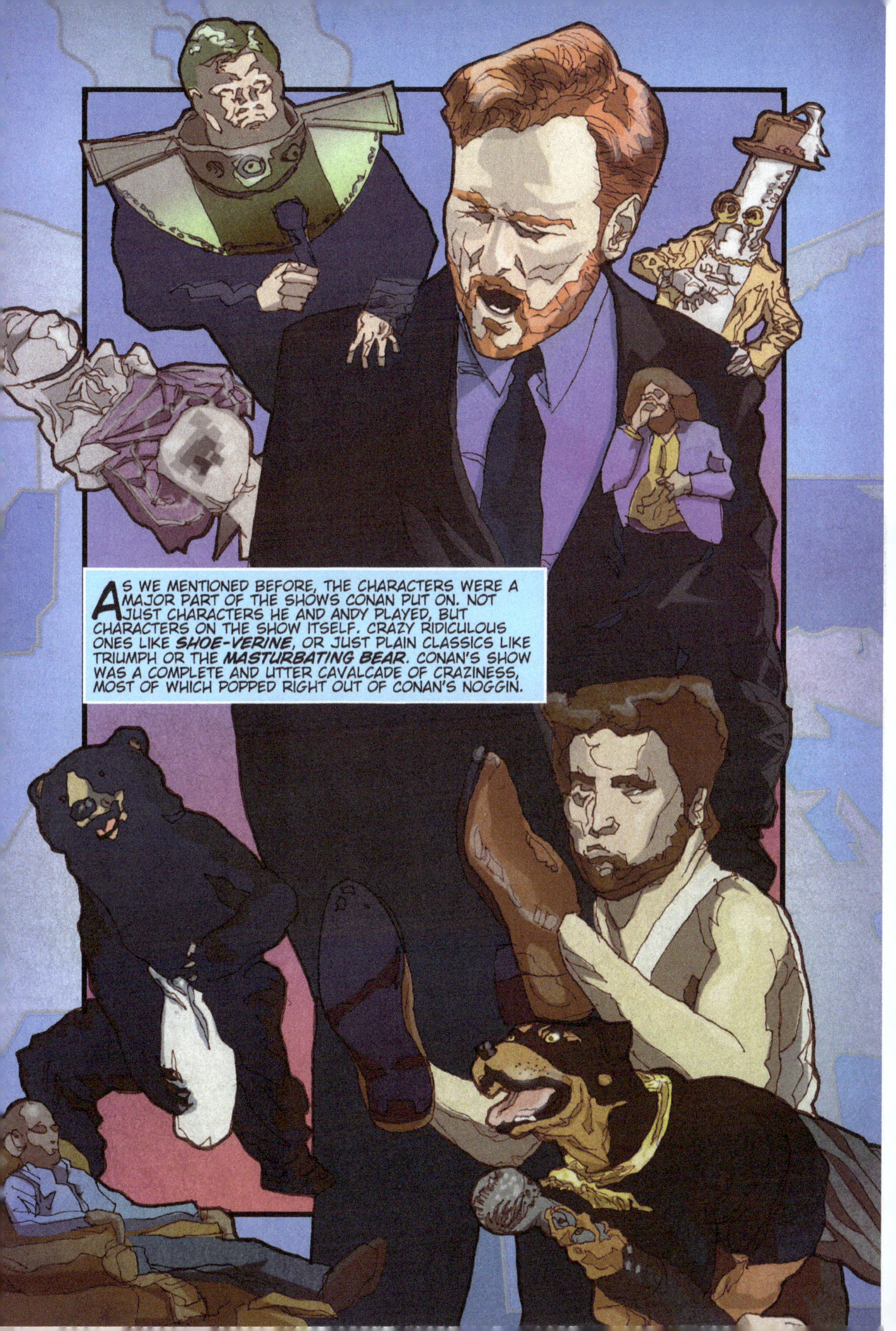
AS WE MENTIONED BEFORE, THE CHARACTERS WERE A MAJOR PART OF THE SHOWS CONAN PUT ON. NOT JUST CHARACTERS HE AND ANDY PLAYED, BUT CHARACTERS ON THE SHOW ITSELF. CRAZY RIDICULOUS ONES LIKE SHOE-VERINE, OR JUST PLAIN CLASSICS LIKE TRIUMPH OR THE MASTURBATING BEAR. CONAN'S SHOW WAS A COMPLETE AND UTTER CAVALCADE OF CRAZINESS, MOST OF WHICH POPPED RIGHT OUT OF CONAN'S NOGGIN.

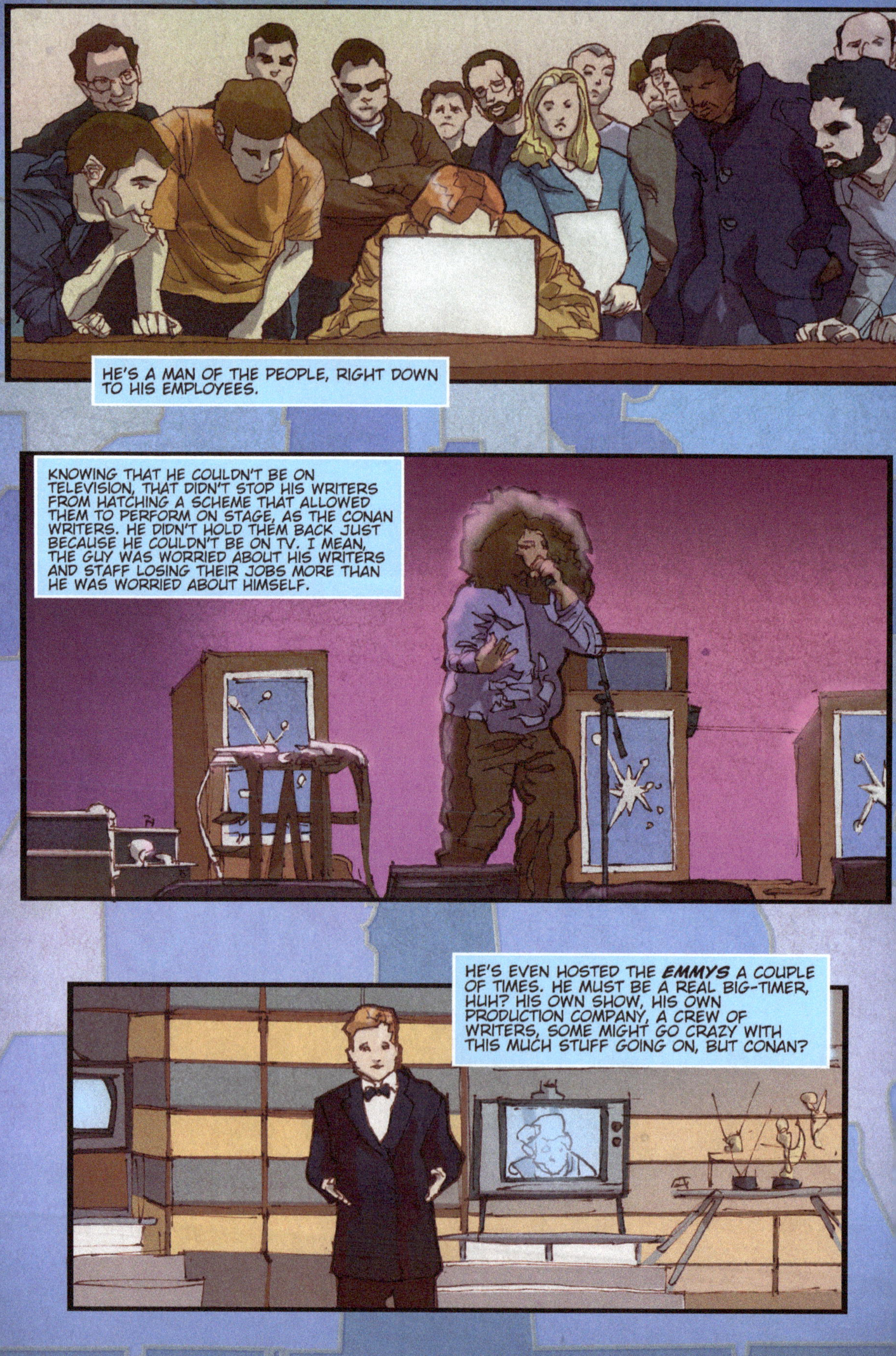
HE'S A MAN OF THE PEOPLE, RIGHT DOWN TO HIS EMPLOYEES.
KNOWING THAT HE COULDN'T BE ON TELEVISION, THAT DIDN'T STOP HIS WRITERS FROM HATCHING A SCHEME THAT ALLOWED THEM TO PERFORM ON STAGE, AS THE CONAN WRITERS. HE DIDN'T HOLD THEM BACK JUST BECAUSE HE COULDN'T BE ON TV. I MEAN, THE GUY WAS WORRIED ABOUT HIS WRITERS AND STAFF LOSING THEIR JOBS MORE THAN HE WAS WORRIED ABOUT HIMSELF.
HE'S EVEN HOSTED THE ***EMMYS*** A COUPLE OF TIMES. HE MUST BE A REAL BIG-TIMER, HUH? HIS OWN SHOW, HIS OWN PRODUCTION COMPANY, A CREW OF WRITERS, SOME MIGHT GO CRAZY WITH THIS MUCH STUFF GOING ON, BUT CONAN?

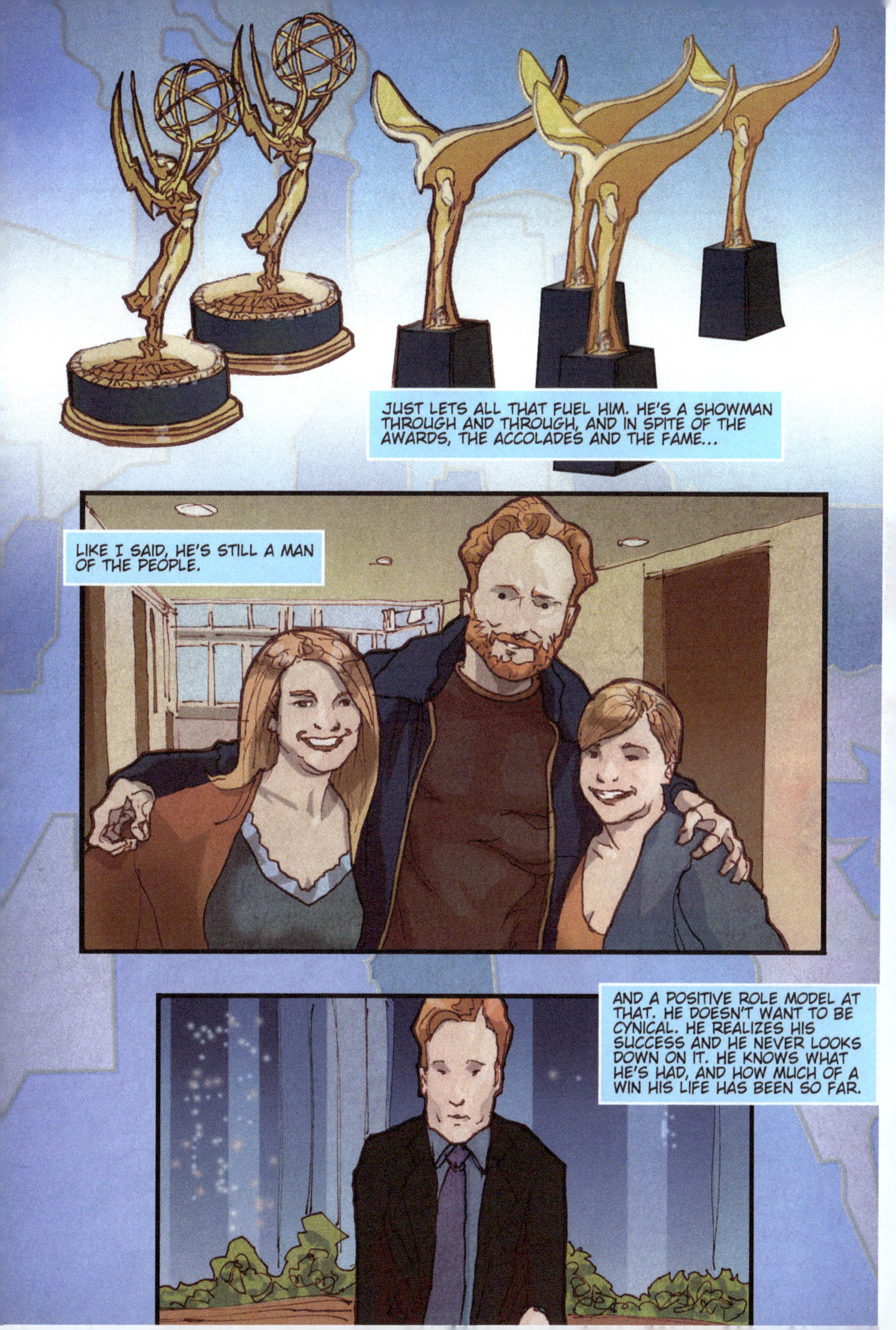
JUST LETS ALL THAT FUEL HIM. HE'S A SHOWMAN THROUGH AND THROUGH, AND IN SPITE OF THE AWARDS, THE ACCOLADES AND THE FAME...
LIKE I SAID, HE'S STILL A MAN OF THE PEOPLE.
AND A POSITIVE ROLE MODEL AT THAT. HE DOESN'T WANT TO BE CYNICAL. HE REALIZES HIS SUCCESS AND HE NEVER LOOKS DOWN ON IT. HE KNOWS WHAT HE'S HAD, AND HOW MUCH OF A WIN HIS LIFE HAS BEEN SO FAR.

FAME
Conan O'Brien

CW Cooke & Patrick McCormack — Writers

Erick Adrian Marquez — Penciler

Erick Adrian Marquez — Colorist

Warren Montgomery — Letterer

Darren G. Davis — Graphics

Darren G. Davis
Publisher

Jason Schultz
Vice President

Hayden Cowan
Coordinator

Jarred Weisfeld
Literary Manager

Kailey Marsh
Entertainment Manager

Maggie Jessup
Publicity

Janda Tithia
Coordinator

John Shableski
Sales Director

Atom Freeman
Consultant

Vonnie Harris
New Business

Adam Ellis
Coordinator

Chad Jones
Production

www.bluewaterprod.com

FAME AND CONTENTS ARE COPYRIGHT © AND ™ DARREN G. DAVIS. ALL RIGHTS RESERVED. BLUEWATER COMICS IS COPYRIGHT © AND ™ DARREN G. DAVIS. ALL RIGHTS RESERVED. ANY REPRODUCTION OF THIS MATERIAL IS STRICTLY PROHIBITED IN ANY MEDIA FORM OTHER THAN FOR PROMOTIONAL PURPOSES UNLESS DARREN G. DAVIS OR BLUEWATER COMICS GIVES WRITTEN CONSENT.
www.bluewaterprod.com

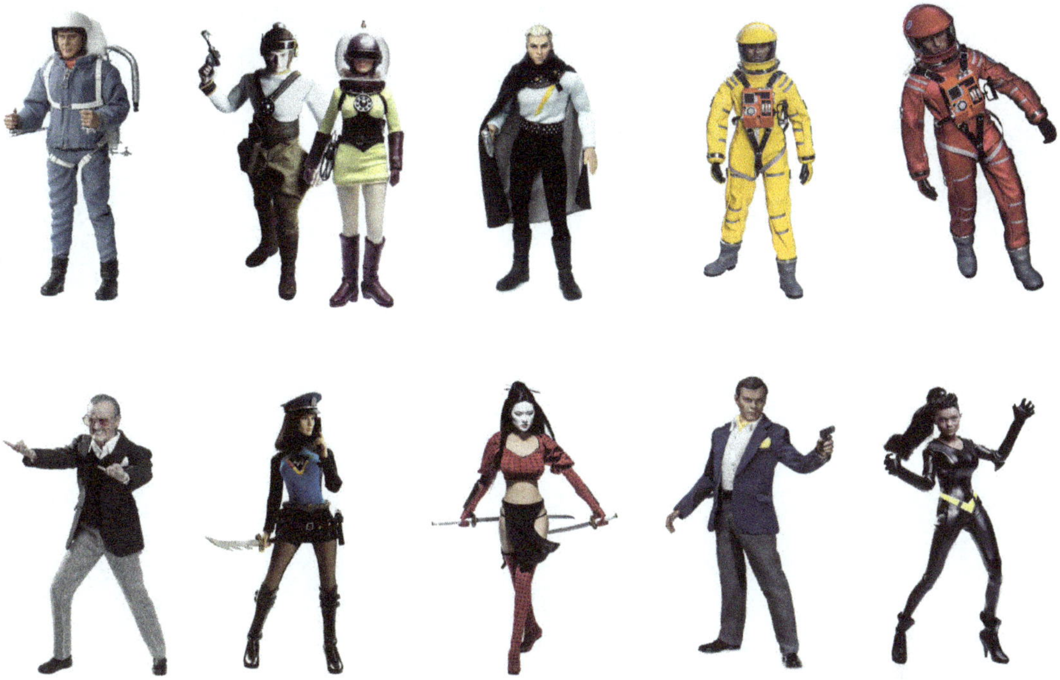

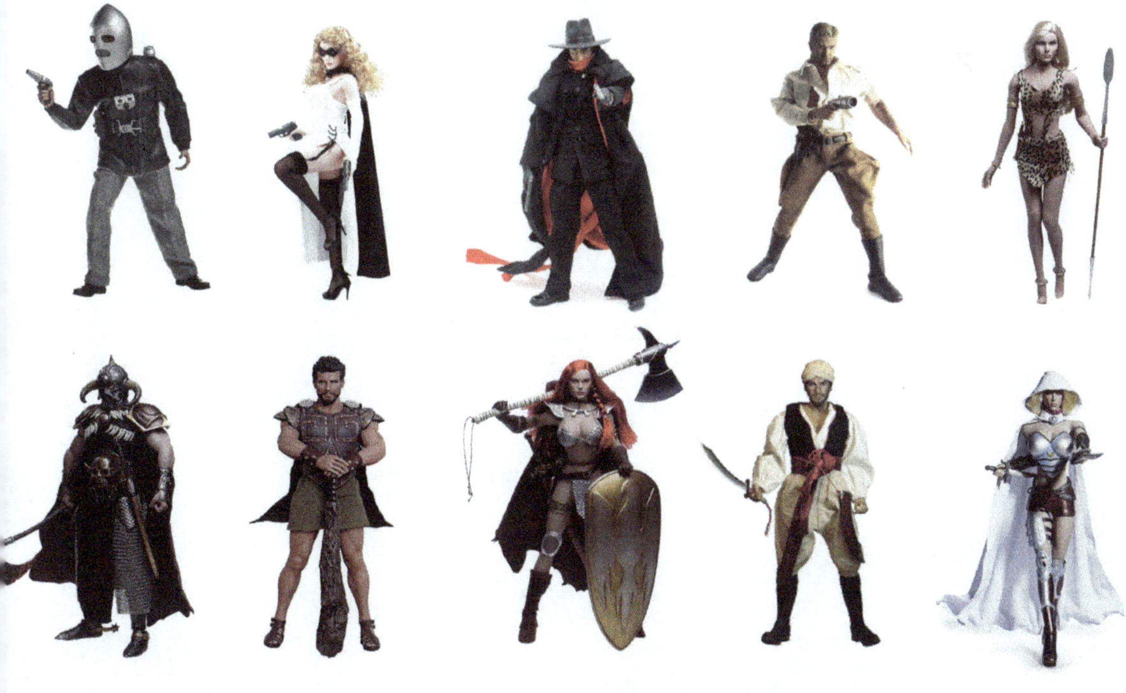

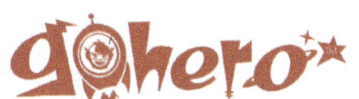

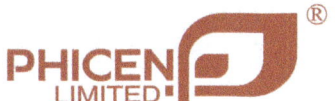

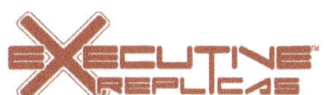

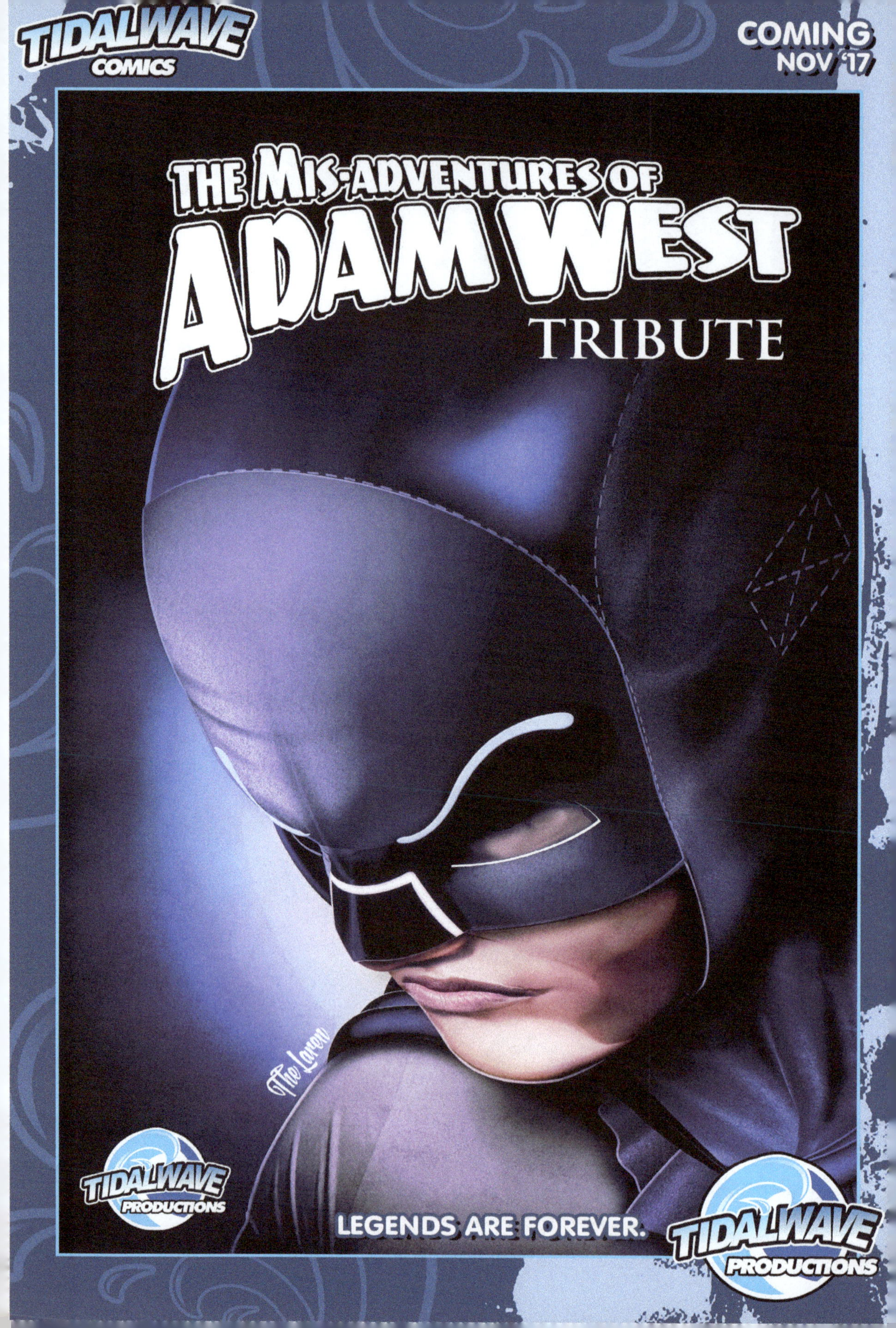

TIDALWAVE COMICS
COMING NOV '17
THE MIS-ADVENTURES OF ADAM WEST
TRIBUTE
TIDALWAVE PRODUCTIONS
LEGENDS ARE FOREVER.
TIDALWAVE PRODUCTIONS

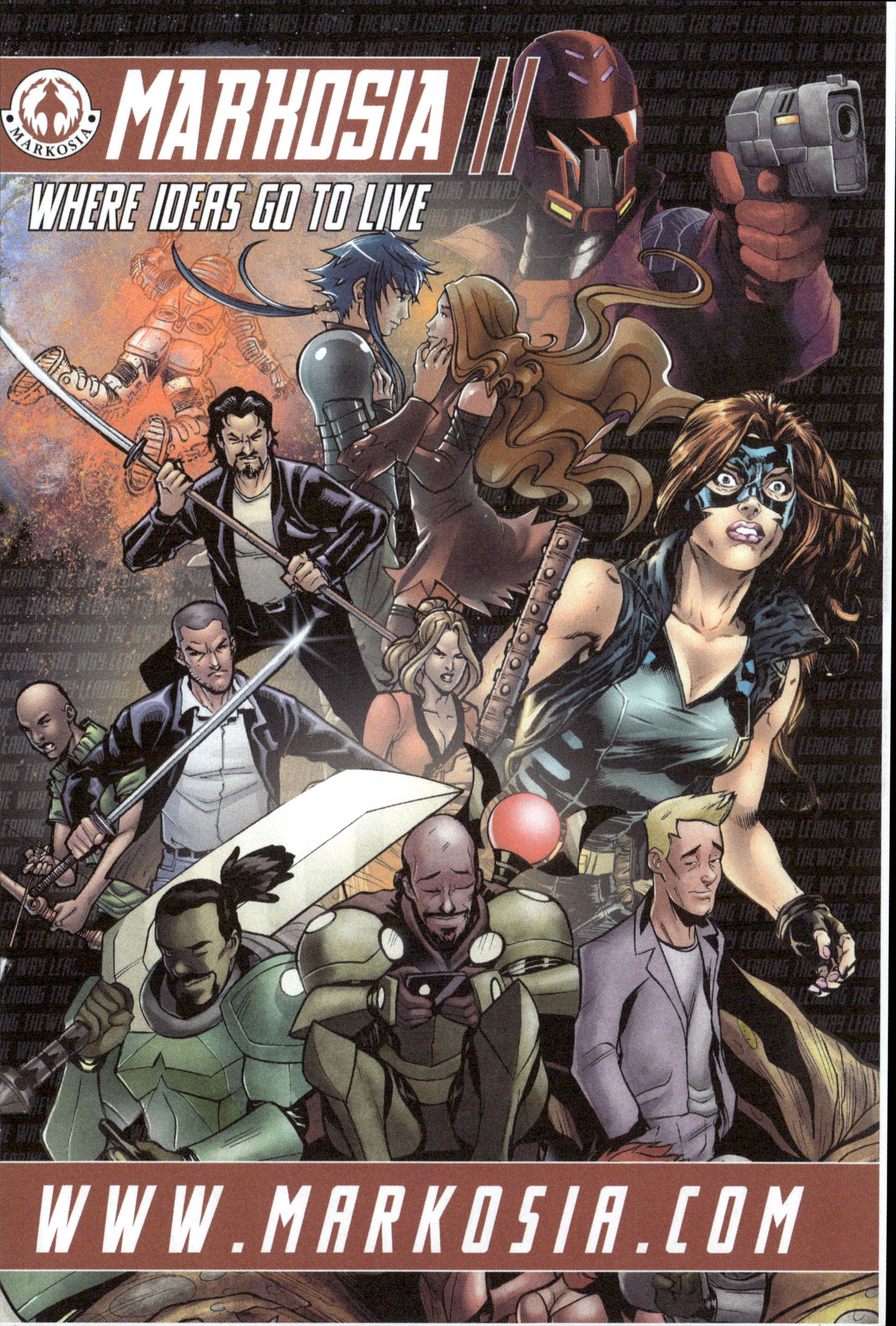
MARKOSIA
MARKOSIA
WHERE IDEAS GO TO LIVE
WWW.MARKOSIA.COM

#ERASEHATE WITH THE MATTHEW SHEPARD FOUNDATION

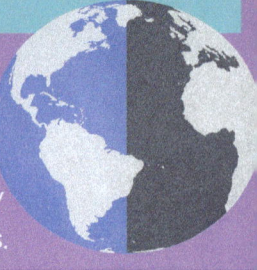

With your donated dollars and volunteer hours, we work tirelessly to erase hate from every corner of America through our programs.

SPEAKING ENGAGEMENTS

Since Matt's death in 1998, Judy and Dennis have been determined to prevent others from similar tragedies. By sharing their story, they are able to carry on Matt's legacy.

HATE CRIMES REPORTING

Our work to improve reporting includes conducting trainings for law enforcement agencies, building relationships between community leaders and law enforcement, and developing policy reform in reporting practices.

LARAMIE PROJECT

MSF offers support to productions of The Laramie Project, which depicts the events leading up to and after Matt's murder. It remains one of the most performed plays in America.

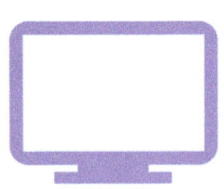

MATTHEW'S PLACE

MatthewsPlace.com is a blog designed to provide young LGBTQ+ people with an outlet for their voices. From finance to health to love and dating, and everything in between, our writers contribute excellent material.

Erase Hate

Matthew Shepard Foundation
embracing diversity

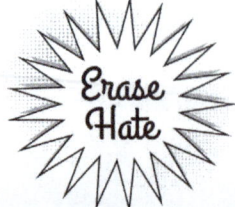

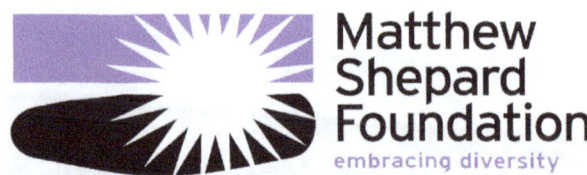

CPSIA information can be obtained
at www.ICGtesting.com
Printed in the USA
BVHW062257211221
624600BV00002B/27